AVIATION WEATHER

AC 00-6B

U.S. Department of Transportation
From AC 00-6B

Published by

Unmanned Publishing
Hazard, Kentucky
www.unmannedpublishing.com

AVIATION WEATHER: AC 00-6B © 2018 by Unmanned Publishing, Inc.

This publication contains an FAA Publication published on August 23, 2016 and is current as of January 01, 2018.

None of the material in this publication supersedes any documents, procedures, or regulations issued by the Federal Aviation Administration. Unmanned Publishing does not claim copywrite on any material published herein that was taken from United States government resources. The government documents reprinted herein are exact facsimiles of original publications

All rights reserved. No part of this book may be reproduced in any form or by any electronic, mechanical, or photocopying means including information storage and retrieval systems, without permission in writing from the publisher. The only exception is by a reviewer, who may quote short excerpts in a review or editorial article.

While the advice and information in this book are believed to be true and accurate at the date of publication, the publisher makes no warranty, express or implied, and no patent liability is assumed with respect to the use of the information for damages resulting from the use of the information contained herein. Although every precaution has been taken in the preparation of this book, the publisher, editors, and author assume no responsibility for errors or omissions.

Designations used by companies to distinguish their products are often claimed as trademarks. All brand names and product names used in this book are trade names, service marks, trademarks or registered trademarks of their respective owners. The publisher is not associated with any product or vendor mentioned in this book.

Edited by Chris Stiles

Cover designed by Bart Massey

Printed in the United States of America

First Printing: January 2018
Unmanned Publishing, Inc.
www.unmannedpublishing.com

ISBN: 978-1-9768992-1-8

Introduction

It is our pleasure to present this first edition of the Aviation Weather: AC 00-6B. This FAA advisory circular provides weather knowledge considered essential for most pilots. It is intended to provide basic weather information that all airmen must know, and to be used as a resource for pilot and dispatcher training programs. This publication supplements its companion manual, the current edition of AC 00-45H Aviation Weather Services, which explains U.S. aviation weather products and services.

This handbook is part of a series of resources developed specially for the Unmanned Aircraft System (UAS) industry, and was birthed out of an unsuccessful search for suitable texts and resources for professionals and businesses in the industry. Series authors are drawn from within the UAS industry, professionals operating in specialties in the field, as well as from universities and learning institutions from around the world.

While Unmanned Aircraft Systems are so named by the FAA, they are also commonly referred to by other names such as drones, quadcopters, multirotors, UAVs, Remotely Piloted Aircraft, ect. Unmanned Aircraft are everywhere nowadays, and they have become part of everyday life for so many people and businesses. As the technologies inside them have advanced and prices have dropped, the availability of these systems has increased, making it more affordable and easier for professionals to implement the use of UAS in daily operations. This ranges from aerial videography for real estate, to construction management, surveying, facility inspections, and so much more. It is well understood that the UAS industry is a highly dynamic and constantly evolving field that is projected to see explosive growth within the next decade. Potential uses are only limited by your imagination.

ABOUT THE CONTRIBUTORS:

CHRIS STILES (EDITOR) - Has been involved with unmanned aircraft for 15 years in varying capacitors, and has been a rated UAS flight instructor since 2005. He started flying medium sized fixed wing UAS in the Army, working in military intelligence and has subsequently spent 6 years overseas supporting counter-terrorism operations in the middle-east and counter-drug operations in central America. With experience on over two dozen UAS systems varying in size from 0.5 – 3,000 lbs. and operating a variety of specialized payloads and sensors in every type of environment imaginable, there is very little that he hasn't done in the field. Chris has conducted 9,000+ flight hours supporting all sectors of the drone market from active duty service in the U.S. Army, as a defense contractor, academia, public/civil agency support, to commercial business sector operations. Mr. Stiles' UAS experience includes conducting flight instruction, maintenance & repair, piloting & sensor operations, system & sensor research & development, general government contracting as well as logistical, analysis, and programmatic support, technical writing, and safety & program development. He has also helped academic institutions develop training programs and conduct research with unmanned aircraft, has authored a multitude of technical publications, occasionally speaks at conferences, and actively promotes UAS education, adoption, as well as proper legislation for the technology. He has also been involved with multiple startup companies in executive leadership positions, and is a key advisor for a couple other UAS startups. One of his companies, Unmanned Services, Inc. was an early company to apply for and receive a Section 333 Exemption from the FAA, and was also one of the first entities granted a night flight waiver. He has instructed and mentored thousands of students, to include teaching hundreds of students in FAA Part 107 test prep courses since early 2016.

BART MASSEY M.Ed. (COVER DESIGN, PROOFREADER) - Bart has a diverse background ranging from technical innovations to international winemaking medals. He has a Master's Degree in Adult & Higher Education, and is a professional photographer that has worked in seven countries and has been President and CEO of multiple companies in his career thus far. Bart is also a public speaker that integrates, success, attitude, grit, timing, and locating the correct professionals to become involved in successful endeavors. He discusses how to recognize talent and be able to motivate and reward them for their efforts. He has been writing specialty books on various subjects in various fields since 1996, such as for hospitals, computer specialists and police agencies. Manuals were created from these books to train or re-train over 1000 employees. Bart recruited, hired, trained and deployed teams of trainers across multiple states in order to provide the training in a professional and timely manner. He has since developed curriculum for multiple college classes, workforce training and has educated more than 600 participants in classes ranging from "UAS 107 Certification Preparation" to "Building Your Own Drone". Bart is a Licensed Remote Pilot and is the Executive Director of the USA Drone Port. The nation's first non-profit drone facility used to train, invent, innovate, develop and manufacture unmanned robotics. The USA Drone Port is the catalyst for entrepreneurs, educators, students and innovators. In the fall of 2017 he organized and led the first team to have a live UAS integration into Search and Rescue in the state of Kentucky. This event included three helicopters, seven UAS Pilots, five fire and rescue departments, land based rescue vehicles and many spectators and facilitators.

UNMANNED PUBLISHING - Provides educational resources for the unmanned and robotics systems industry. Our authors are experts in their respective fields and many are pilots, college educators, and previous authors with years of technical experience in their respective subject matter. Our high standards dictate that all authors and contributors to each work be vetted for their expertise in order to provide our readers with the highest quality of knowledge. Our authors are not merely college educators with theoretical knowledge, and have little to no actual field experience on the subject. They live and operate in the actual world of unmanned systems and robotics, and have real knowledge to pass on to benefit our readers.

WE WOULD LIKE TO HEAR FROM YOU

We value your opinion and want to know what we are doing right, what we could do better, as well as what topics you would like to see us publish about.

We welcome your comments. Please consider reviewing this book by visiting it's listing on Amazon.com. You can also email us to let us know what you did or didn't like about this book—as well as what we can do to make our books better, or any mistakes contained herein. Please list your name and location as we may feature your review on our website or newsletters

BULK SALES

Unmanned Publishing offers excellent discounts on this book when ordered in quantity for bulk purchases or special sales. For more information, please contact us at info@unmannedpublishing.com.

OTHER AUTHORS AND CONTENT CREATORS

If you are an author or content creator, or would like to be one, we are here to help you out. We can help you in any manner in getting works published online, or in physical print and distributed. We can also assist with other types of digital and video media creation. Please contact us at info@unmannedpublishing.com.

ADDITIONAL SUPPORT, eBOOKS, DISCOUNT OFFERS, AND MORE

New editions of this book will be published as the FAA releases updates to this publication in order to keep Remote Pilots informed on any Regulatory and Policy changes.

Please email us for technical support for any of our published works at info@unmannedpublishing.com

Unmanned Publishing offers eBook and printed versions of all our published works on our website at www.unmannedpublishing.com, as well as on www.amazon.com

Since you have purchased this printed work, Unmanned Publishing offers a 10% discount on eBook versions in any format you prefer. Please email info@unmannedpublishing.com, and specify the eBook file format you need with the code: AW3518

You can also receive a 10% discount on future eBook or printed editions of this book by emailing info@unmannedpublishing.com, and specifying the edition version and format in which you would like to purchase using the discount code: AW3518+

Subscribe to our newsletter for free updates on future edition releases, delivery of free resources strait to your inbox, and other resources we publish on our website at www.unmannedpublishing.com.

Stay informed with Unmanned Publishing's online resources by visiting our website to sign up for free publication updates and follow us on our social media pages at:

U.S. Department of Transportation
Federal Aviation Administration

Advisory Circular

Subject: Aviation Weather	Date: 8/23/16	AC No: 00-6B
	Initiated by: AFS-400	Change:

This advisory circular (AC) was published by the Federal Aviation Administration (FAA) Flight Standards Service (AFS), with contributions from the National Weather Service (NWS). The publication began in 1943 as CAA Bulletin No. 25, Meteorology for Pilots, which at the time contained weather knowledge considered essential for most pilots. As aircraft flew farther, faster, and higher, and as meteorological knowledge grew, the bulletin became obsolete. It was revised in 1954 under a new title, The Pilots' Weather Handbook, and updated again in 1965. In 1975 it was revised under its current title.

Previous editions have suffered one common problem—they dealt in part with weather services that continually change, in keeping with current techniques and service demands. As a result, each edition was somewhat outdated almost as soon as it was published, its obsolescence growing throughout the period it remained in print.

In 1975, in order to alleviate this problem, the authors completely rewrote the AC. They streamlined it into a clear, concise, readable book, and omitted all reference to specific weather services.

The 1975 text remained valid and adequate for many years. Its companion manual, the current edition of AC 00-45, Aviation Weather Services, supplements this AC. In 2015, this supplement was updated concurrently with this text. This was done to reflect changes brought about by new products and services, particularly since this information is now available through the Internet. The companion AC describes current weather services and formats, and uses real world examples of weather graphics and text products.

The two manuals can be downloaded for free via the Internet in PDF format. Print versions are also sold separately at nominal cost, allowing pilots the opportunity to own a reference copy of the supplement to keep current with aviation weather services.

New scientific capabilities now necessitate an update to this AC. In 1975, aviation users were not directly touched by radar and satellite weather. In 2016, much of what airmen understand about the current atmosphere comes from these important data sources. This AC is intended to provide basic weather information that all airmen must know. This document is intended to be used as a resource for pilot and dispatcher training programs.

This AC cancels AC 00-6A, Aviation Weather for Pilots and Flight Operations Personnel.

John Barbagallo
Deputy Director, Flight Standards Service

CONTENTS

Paragraph **Page**

Chapter 1. The Earth's Atmosphere 1-1
    1.1 Introduction 1-1
    1.2 Composition 1-1
        1.2.1   Air Parcel 1-2
    1.3 Vertical Structure 1-2
        1.3.1   Troposphere 1-2
        1.3.2   Stratosphere 1-3
        1.3.3   Mesosphere 1-4
        1.3.4   Thermosphere 1-5
        1.3.5   Exosphere 1-5
    1.4 The Standard Atmosphere 1-5

Chapter 2. Heat and Temperature 2-1
    2.1 Introduction 2-1
    2.2 Matter 2-1
    2.3 Energy 2-1
    2.4 Heat 2-1
    2.5 Temperature 2-1
        2.5.1   Temperature Measurement 2-1
        2.5.2   Temperature Scales 2-1
    2.6 Heat Transfer 2-3
        2.6.1   Radiation 2-3
        2.6.2   Conduction 2-6
        2.6.3   Convection 2-7
    2.7 Thermal Response 2-8
    2.8 Temperature Variations with Altitude 2-11
        2.8.1   Atmospheric Sounding 2-12
        2.8.2   Isothermal Layer 2-12
        2.8.3   Temperature Inversion 2-12

Chapter 3. Water Vapor 3-1
   3.1 Introduction 3-1
   3.2 The Hydrologic Cycle 3-1
         3.2.1   Evaporation 3-2
         3.2.2   Transpiration 3-2
         3.2.3   Sublimation 3-2
         3.2.4   Condensation 3-2
         3.2.5   Transportation 3-2
         3.2.6   Precipitation 3-2
         3.2.7   Runoff 3-2
         3.2.8   Infiltration 3-2
         3.2.9   Groundwater Flow 3-3
         3.2.10 Plant Uptake 3-3
   3.3 Saturation 3-3
   3.4 Relative Humidity 3-3
   3.5 Dewpoint 3-4
   3.6 Temperature-Dewpoint Spread (Dewpoint Depression) 3-4
   3.7 Change of Phase 3-5
         3.7.1   Latent Heat 3-5

Chapter 4. Earth-Atmosphere Heat Imbalances 4-1
   4.1 Introduction 4-1
   4.2 The Earth-Atmosphere Energy Balance 4-1
   4.3 Heat Imbalances Between Earth's Surface and the Atmosphere 4-3
         4.3.1   Sensible Heating 4-3
         4.3.2   Latent Heat 4-4
   4.4 Heat Imbalance Variations with Latitude 4-4
   4.5 Seasons 4-5
   4.6 Diurnal Temperature Variation 4-7

Chapter 5. Atmospheric Pressure and Altimetry 5-1
   5.1 Introduction 5-1

5.2 Atmospheric Pressure 5-1
    5.2.1 Barometer 5-2
    5.2.2 Atmospheric Pressure Units 5-2
    5.2.3 Station Pressure 5-3
    5.2.4 Pressure Variation 5-3
    5.2.5 Sea Level Pressure 5-5
    5.2.6 Constant Pressure Surface 5-7
5.3 Density 5-10
    5.3.1 Volume Effects on Density 5-10
    5.3.2 Changes in Density 5-11
    5.3.3 Density Effects on Pressure 5-11
    5.3.4 Temperature Effects on Density 5-12
    5.3.5 Water Vapor Effects on Density 5-12
5.4 Altimetry 5-13
    5.4.1 Altitude 5-13
5.5 Density Altitude 5-16

Chapter 6. Weather Charts 6-1
6.1 Introduction 6-1
6.2 Weather Observation Sources 6-1
6.3 Analysis 6-2
    6.3.1 Analysis Procedure 6-2
6.4 Surface Chart 6-6
6.5 Constant Pressure Chart 6-7

Chapter 7. Wind 7-1
7.1 Introduction 7-1
7.2 Naming of the Wind 7-1
7.3 Forces That Affect the Wind 7-1
    7.3.1 Pressure Gradient Force (PGF) 7-1
    7.3.2 Coriolis Force 7-2
    7.3.3 Friction Force 7-4
7.4 Upper Air Wind 7-5
7.5 Surface Wind 7-6

Chapter 8. Global Circulations and Jet Streams 8-1
    8.1 Non-Rotating Earth Circulation System 8-1
    8.2 Rotating Earth Circulation System 8-1
    8.3 Jet Streams 8-2
        8.3.1   Introduction 8-2
        8.3.2   Direction of Wind Flow 8-3
        8.3.3   Location 8-4

Chapter 9. Local Winds 9-1
    9.1 Description 9-1
    9.2 Hazards 9-2
    9.3 Sea Breeze 9-2
        9.3.1   Sea Breeze Front 9-3
        9.3.2   Effects of Coastline Shape 9-3
    9.4 Land Breeze 9-4
    9.5 Lake Breeze 9-5
    9.6 Valley Breeze 9-7
    9.7 Mountain-Plains Wind System 9-8
    9.8 Mountain Breeze 9-9

Chapter 10. Air Masses, Fronts, and the Wave Cyclone Model 10-1
    10.1 Air Masses 10-1
        10.1.1   Air Mass Classification 10-1
        10.1.2   Air Mass Modification 10-2
    10.2 Fronts 10-3
    10.3 The Wave Cyclone Model 10-7
    10.4 Dryline 10-9

Chapter 11. Vertical Motion and Cloud Formation 11-1
    11.1 Introduction 11-1
    11.2 Vertical Motion Effects on an Unsaturated Air Parcel 11-1
    11.3 Vertical Motion Effects on a Saturated Air Parcel 11-2
    11.4 Common Sources of Vertical Motion 11-5
        11.4.1   Orographic Effects 11-5
        11.4.2   Frictional Effects 11-6

11.4.3	Frontal Lift	11-6
11.4.4	Buoyancy	11-7

Chapter 12. Atmospheric Stability 12-1
   12.1 Introduction 12-1
   12.2 Using a Parcel as a Tool to Evaluate Stability 12-1
   12.3 Stability Types 12-1
      12.3.1 Absolute Stability 12-1
      12.3.2 Neutral Stability 12-2
      12.3.3 Absolute Instability 12-3
      12.3.4 Conditional Instability 12-4
      12.3.5 Summary of Stability Types 12-6
   12.4 Processes that Change Atmospheric Stability 12-7
      12.4.1 Wind Effects on Stability 12-7
      12.4.2 Vertical Air Motion Effects on Stability 12-7
      12.4.3 Diurnal Temperature Variation Effects on Stability 12-8
   12.5 Measurements of Stability 12-9
      12.5.1 Lifted Index 12-9
      12.5.2 Convective Available Potential Energy 12-10
   12.6 Summary 12-11

Chapter 13. Clouds 13-1
   13.1 Introduction 13-1
   13.2 Cloud Forms 13-1
   13.3 Cloud Levels 13-2
   13.4 Cloud Types 13-2
      13.4.1 High Clouds 13-2
      13.4.2 Middle Clouds 13-5
      13.4.3 Low Clouds 13-9

Chapter 14. Precipitation 14-1
   14.1 Introduction 14-1
   14.2 Necessary Ingredients for Formation 14-1
   14.3 Growth Process 14-1
   14.4 Precipitation Types 14-3

Chapter 15. Adverse Wind 15-1
15.1 Introduction 15-1
15.2 Crosswind 15-1
15.3 Gust 15-1
15.4 Tailwind 15-2
15.5 Variable Wind/Sudden Wind Shift 15-2
15.6 Wind Shear 15-2

Chapter 16. Weather, Obstructions to Visibility, Low Ceiling, and Mountain Obscuration 16-1
16.1 Weather and Obstructions to Visibility 16-1
    16.1.1   Fog 16-1
    16.1.2   Mist 16-5
    16.1.3   Haze 16-5
    16.1.4   Smoke 16-5
    16.1.5   Precipitation 16-5
    16.1.6   Blowing Snow 16-6
    16.1.7   Dust Storm 16-6
    16.1.8   Sandstorm 16-6
    16.1.9   Volcanic Ash 16-7
16.2 Low Ceiling and Mountain Obscuration 16-8
    16.2.1   Low Ceiling 16-8
    16.2.2   Mountain Obscuration 16-9

Chapter 17. Turbulence 17-1
17.1 Introduction 17-1
17.2 Causes of Turbulence 17-1
    17.2.1   Convective Turbulence 17-1
    17.2.2   Mechanical Turbulence 17-3
    17.2.3   Wind Shear Turbulence 17-5
17.3 Turbulence Factors 17-6

Chapter 18. Icing 18-1
18.1 Introduction 18-1
18.2 Supercooled Water 18-1

18.3 Structural Icing 18-1
    18.3.1 Rime Icing 18-1
    18.3.2 Clear Icing 18-1
    18.3.3 Mixed Icing 18-2
    18.3.4 Icing Factors 18-2
    18.3.5 Icing in Stratiform Clouds 18-4
    18.3.6 Icing in Cumuliform Clouds 18-4
    18.3.7 Icing with Fronts 18-4
    18.3.8 Icing with Mountains 18-5
    18.3.9 Icing Hazards 18-6
18.4 Engine Icing. 18-7
    18.4.1 Carburetor Icing 18-7
    18.4.2 High Ice Water Content (HIWC) 18-7

Chapter 19. Thunderstorms 19-1
  19.1 Introduction 19-1
  19.2 Necessary Ingredients for Thunderstorm Cell Formation 19-1
  19.3 Thunderstorm Cell Life Cycle 19-1
  19.4 Thunderstorm Types 19-2
  19.5 Factors that Influence Thunderstorm Motion 19-5
  19.6 Hazards 19-6
    19.6.1 Lightning 19-6
    19.6.2 Adverse Wind 19-6
    19.6.3 Downburst 19-6
    19.6.4 Turbulence 19-8
    19.6.5 Icing 19-8
    19.6.6 Hail 19-9
    19.6.7 Rapid Altimeter Changes 19-10
    19.6.8 Static Electricity 19-10
    19.6.9 Tornado 19-10

Chapter 20. Weather Radar 20-1

20.1 Principles of Weather Radar 20-1

- 20.1.1 Antenna 20-1
- 20.1.2 Backscattered Energy 20-1
- 20.1.3 Power Output 20-2
- 20.1.4 Wavelengths 20-2
- 20.1.5 Attenuation 20-3
- 20.1.6 Resolution 20-4
- 20.1.7 Wave Propagation 20-7
- 20.1.8 Intensity of Precipitation 20-9

Chapter 21. Tropical Weather 21-1

21.1 Circulation 21-1

- 21.1.1 Subtropical High Pressure Belts 21-1
- 21.1.2 Trade Wind Belts 21-3
- 21.1.3 The Intertropical Convergence Zone (ITCZ) 21-5
- 21.1.4 Monsoon 21-5

21.2 Transitory Systems 21-7

- 21.2.1 Remnants of Polar Fronts and Shear Lines 21-7
- 21.2.2 Tropical Upper Tropospheric Trough (TUTT) 21-8
- 21.2.3 Tropical Wave 21-9
- 21.2.4 West African Disturbance Line (WADL) 21-10
- 21.2.5 Tropical Cyclones 21-11

Chapter 22. Arctic Weather 22-1

22.1 Introduction 22-1

22.2 Climate, Air Masses, and Fronts 22-1

- 22.2.1 Long Days and Nights 22-2
- 22.2.2 Land and Water 22-2
- 22.2.3 Temperature 22-2
- 22.2.4 Clouds and Precipitation 22-2
- 22.2.5 Wind 22-3
- 22.2.6 Air Masses—Winter 22-3

22.2.7 Air Masses—Summer 22-3
22.2.8 Fronts 22-3
22.3 Arctic Peculiarities 22-3
22.3.1 Effects of Temperature Inversion 22-3
22.3.2 Light Reflection by Snow-Covered Surfaces 22-3
22.3.3 Light from Celestial Bodies 22-3
22.4 Weather Hazards 22-4
22.4.1 Fog and Ice Fog 22-4
22.4.2 Blowing and Drifting Snow 22-4
22.4.3 Frost 22-4
22.4.4 Whiteout 22-4

Chapter 23. Space Weather 23-1
23.1 The Sun—Prime Source of Space Weather 23-1
23.2 The Sun's Energy Output and Variability 23-1
23.3 Sunspots and the Solar Cycle 23-1
23.4 Solar Wind 23-1
23.5 Solar Eruptive Activity 23-2
23.6 Geospace 23-2
23.7 Galactic Cosmic Radiation 23-3
23.8 Geomagnetic Storms 23-4
23.9 Solar Radiation Storms 23-4
23.10 Ionospheric Storms 23-5
23.11 Solar Flare Radio Blackouts 23-5
23.12 Effects of Space Weather on Aircraft Operations 23-6
23.12.1 Communications 23-6
23.12.2 Navigation and Global Positioning System (GPS) 23-6
23.12.3 Radiation Exposure to Flight Crews and Passengers 23-6
23.12.4 Radiation Effects on Avionics 23-6

List of Figures

Figure 1-1.	Vertical Structure of the Atmosphere	1-4
Figure 1-2.	U.S. Standard Atmosphere within the Troposphere	1-6
Figure 2-1.	Comparison of Kelvin, Celsius, and Fahrenheit Temperature Scales	2-3
Figure 2-2.	Radiation Example	2-4
Figure 2-3.	Temperature's Effect on Radiation Wavelength	2-5
Figure 2-4.	Solar Zenith Angle	2-6
Figure 2-5.	Heat Transfer Examples	2-8
Figure 2-6.	Specific Heat Capacity: Water Versus Sand	2-10
Figure 2-7.	Variation of Mean Daily Temperatures for San Francisco (Maritime) and Kansas City (Continental)	2-11
Figure 2-8.	Sounding with an Isothermal Layer	2-12
Figure 2-9.	Sounding with a Temperature Inversion	2-13
Figure 3-1.	The Hydrologic Cycle	3-1
Figure 3-2.	Temperature Effects on Relative Humidity	3-4
Figure 3-3.	Temperature-Dewpoint Spread Effect on Relative Humidity	3-5
Figure 3-4.	Latent Heat Transactions when Water Undergoes Phase Transition	3-6
Figure 4-1.	Earth-Atmosphere Energy Balance	4-1
Figure 4-2.	Greenhouse Effect on Nighttime Radiational Cooling	4-2
Figure 4-3.	Development of a Thermal	4-3
Figure 4-4.	Example of Convection in the Atmosphere	4-4
Figure 4-5.	Solar Zenith Angle Variations with Latitude	4-5
Figure 4-6.	Solar Zenith Angle Variations with Northern Hemisphere Seasons	4-6
Figure 4-7.	Average Seasonal Temperature Variation in the Northern Hemisphere	4-6
Figure 4-8.	Clear Sky Diurnal Temperature and Radiation Variations Over Land	4-7
Figure 5-1.	Air Has Weight	5-1
Figure 5-2.	Aneroid Barometer	5-2
Figure 5-3.	Station Pressure	5-3
Figure 5-4.	Air Pressure in the Standard Atmosphere	5-4
Figure 5-5.	Temperature Effect on Pressure	5-5
Figure 5-6.	Reduction of Station Pressure to Sea Level	5-5
Figure 5-7.	Surface Chart Pressure Patterns	5-7
Figure 5-8.	Weather Balloon and Radiosonde	5-8

Figure 5-9.	500 Millibar Constant Pressure Chart	5-9
Figure 5-10.	Density is Mass (Weight) per Volume	5-10
Figure 5-11.	Volume Effects on Density	5-10
Figure 5-12.	Pressure Effects on Density in the Atmosphere	5-11
Figure 5-13.	Temperature Effects on Density	5-12
Figure 5-14.	Water Vapor Effects on Density	5-12
Figure 5-15.	True Versus Indicated Altitude	5-13
Figure 5-16.	Pressure Change Effects on Altimeter Readings	5-14
Figure 5-17.	Temperature Change Effects on Altimeter Readings	5-15
Figure 5-18.	High Density Altitude Effects on Flight	5-17
Figure 6-1.	Weather Observation Sources	6-1
Figure 6-2.	Analysis Procedure Step 1: Determine the Optimal Contour Interval and Values to be Analyzed	6-3
Figure 6-3.	Analysis Procedure Step 2: Draw the Isopleths and Extrema	6-4
Figure 6-4.	Analysis Procedure Step 3: Interpret Significant Weather Features	6-6
Figure 6-5.	Example of a Surface Chart	6-7
Figure 6-6.	Example of a 500 Millibar Constant Pressure Chart	6-8
Figure 7-1.	Direction of Pressure Gradient Force	7-1
Figure 7-2.	Magnitude of Pressure Gradient Force	7-2
Figure 7-3.	Illustration of Coriolis Force	7-2
Figure 7-4.	Coriolis Force Variations Across the Earth	7-3
Figure 7-5.	Coriolis Force Magnitude Variations with Wind Speed	7-4
Figure 7-6.	Friction Force Magnitude Variations with Terrain Roughness	7-4
Figure 7-7.	Friction Force Magnitude Variations with Wind Speed	7-4
Figure 7-8.	Geostrophic Wind	7-5
Figure 7-9.	Upper Air Wind Flow	7-5
Figure 7-10.	Surface Wind Forces	7-6
Figure 7-11.	Surface Wind Flow	7-6
Figure 8-1.	Non-Rotating, Non-Tilted, Waterless, Earth Circulation System	8-1
Figure 8-2.	Earth Circulation System	8-2
Figure 8-3.	Speed Relative to the Earth's Axis Versus Latitude	8-3
Figure 8-4.	Three Cell Circulations and Jet Stream Location	8-4
Figure 8-5.	Polar and Subtropical Jet Streams	8-4

Figure 8-6.	Jet Stream Wind Speeds	8-5
Figure 9-1.	Local Wind Circulation	9-1
Figure 9-2.	Sea Breeze	9-2
Figure 9-3.	Sea Breeze Front	9-3
Figure 9-4.	Effects of Coastline Shape on a Sea Breeze	9-4
Figure 9-5.	Land Breeze	9-5
Figure 9-6.	Lake Breeze	9-6
Figure 9-7.	Sea Breeze/Lake Breeze Example	9-7
Figure 9-8.	Valley Breeze	9-7
Figure 9-9.	Mountain-Plains Wind System	9-8
Figure 9-10.	Mountain Breeze	9-9
Figure 10-1.	Air Mass Classification	10-2
Figure 10-2.	Air Mass Modification—Warm, Moist Air Mass Moving Over a Cold Surface	10-2
Figure 10-3.	Lake Effect	10-3
Figure 10-4.	Fronts	10-4
Figure 10-5.	Cold Front	10-5
Figure 10-6.	Warm Front	10-5
Figure 10-7.	Stationary Front	10-6
Figure 10-8.	Occluded Front	10-6
Figure 10-9.	Wave Cyclone Model—Stage 1	10-7
Figure 10-10.	Wave Cyclone Model—Stage 2	10-7
Figure 10-11.	Wave Cyclone Model—Stage 3	10-8
Figure 10-12.	Wave Cyclone Model—Stage 4	10-8
Figure 10-13.	Wave Cyclone Model—Stage 5	10-8
Figure 10-14.	Dryline Example	10-9
Figure 11-1.	Unsaturated Ascending/Descending Air Parcel Example	11-2
Figure 11-2.	Ascending Air Parcel that Becomes Saturated Example	11-3
Figure 11-3.	Descending Air Parcel Example	11-4
Figure 11-4.	Orographic Effects Example	11-5
Figure 11-5.	Frictional Effects	11-6
Figure 11-6.	Frontal Lift	11-7
Figure 12-1.	Absolute Stability Example	12-2

Figure 12-2.	Neutral Stability Example	12-3
Figure 12-3.	Absolute Instability Example	12-4
Figure 12-4.	Conditional Instability Example	12-5
Figure 12-5.	Stability Types	12-6
Figure 12-6.	Temperature Lapse Rate Effects on Stability	12-7
Figure 12-7.	Vertical Motion Effects on Stability	12-8
Figure 12-8.	Diurnal Temperature Variation Effects on Stability	12-9
Figure 12-9.	Lifted Index Example	12-10
Figure 13-1.	Cirrus (Ci)	13-3
Figure 13-2.	Cirrocumulus (Cc)	13-4
Figure 13-3.	Cirrostratus (Cs)	13-5
Figure 13-4.	Altocumulus (Ac)	13-6
Figure 13-5.	Altocumulus Standing Lenticular (ACSL)	13-7
Figure 13-6.	Thin Altostratus (As)	13-8
Figure 13-7.	Thick Altostratus (As) or Nimbostratus (Ns)	13-9
Figure 13-8.	Cumulus (Cu) with Little Vertical Development	13-10
Figure 13-9.	Towering Cumulus (TCu)	13-11
Figure 13-10.	Stratocumulus (Sc)	13-12
Figure 13-11.	Stratus (St)	13-13
Figure 13-12.	Stratus Fractus (StFra) and/or Cumulus Fractus (CuFra) of Bad Weather	13-14
Figure 13-13.	Cumulonimbus (Cb) without Anvil	13-15
Figure 13-14.	Cumulonimbus (Cb) with Anvil	13-16
Figure 14-1.	The Collision-Coalescence or Warm Rain Process	14-2
Figure 14-2.	Snow Temperature Environment	14-3
Figure 14-3.	Ice Pellets Temperature Environment	14-3
Figure 14-4.	Freezing Rain Temperature Environment	14-4
Figure 14-5.	Rain Temperature Environment	14-4
Figure 15-1.	Crosswind	15-1
Figure 16-1.	Radiation Fog	16-1
Figure 16-2.	Advection Fog	16-2
Figure 16-3.	Advection Fog Formation	16-3
Figure 16-4.	Frontal Fog Formation	16-4
Figure 16-5.	Haboob	16-7

Figure 16-6.	Layer Aloft Ceiling Versus Indefinite Ceiling	16-9
Figure 17-1.	Convective Turbulence	17-2
Figure 17-2.	Thermals	17-2
Figure 17-3.	Mechanical Turbulence	17-3
Figure 17-4.	Mountain Waves	17-4
Figure 17-5.	Mountain Wave Clouds	17-5
Figure 17-6.	Wind Shear Turbulence	17-5
Figure 17-7.	Wind Shear Turbulence Associated with a Temperature Inversion	17-6
Figure 18-1.	Icing with Fronts	18-5
Figure 18-2.	Icing with Mountains	18-6
Figure 19-1.	Necessary Ingredients for Thunderstorm Cell Formation	19-1
Figure 19-2.	Thunderstorm Cell Life Cycle	19-2
Figure 19-3.	Multicell Cluster Thunderstorm	19-3
Figure 19-4.	Multicell Line Thunderstorm	19-4
Figure 19-5.	Supercell Thunderstorm	19-5
Figure 19-6.	Factors that Influence Thunderstorm Motion	19-5
Figure 19-7.	Downburst Life Cycle	19-7
Figure 19-8.	Landing in a Microburst	19-7
Figure 19-9.	Thunderstorm with Shelf Cloud	19-8
Figure 19-10.	Vivian, South Dakota Record Hailstone	19-9
Figure 20-1.	Radar Antenna	20-1
Figure 20-2.	Backscattered Energy	20-2
Figure 20-3.	Wavelengths	20-3
Figure 20-4.	Precipitation Attenuation	20-3
Figure 20-5.	Precipitation Attenuation Versus Wavelength	20-4
Figure 20-6.	Beam Resolution	20-5
Figure 20-7.	Beam Resolution Comparison Between WSR-88D and Aircraft Weather Radar	20-6
Figure 20-8.	Normal Refraction	20-7
Figure 20-9.	Subrefraction	20-8
Figure 20-10.	Superrefraction	20-8
Figure 20-11.	Ducting	20-9
Figure 20-12.	Reflectivity Associated with Liquid Targets	20-10

Figure 21-1.	Mean Worldwide Surface Pressure Distribution and Prevailing Winds Throughout the World in July	21-2
Figure 21-2.	Mean Worldwide Surface Pressure Distribution and Prevailing Winds Throughout the World in January	21-2
Figure 21-3.	A Shear Line and an Induced Trough Caused by a Polar High Pushing into the Subtropics	21-8
Figure 21-4.	A TUTT Moves Eastward Across the Hawaiian Islands. Extensive Cloudiness Develops East of the Trough	21-9
Figure 21-5.	A Northern Hemisphere Easterly Wave Progressing from A–B	21-10
Figure 21-6.	Vertical Cross Section along Line A–B in Figure 21-5	21-10
Figure 21-7.	The Tracks of Nearly 150 Years of Tropical Cyclones and their Strength Weave Across the Globe	21-12
Figure 21-8.	Radar Image of Hurricane Katrina Observed at New Orleans, Louisiana, on August 29, 2005	21-14
Figure 21-9.	Hurricane Andrew Observed by Satellite in 1992	21-14
Figure 22-1.	The Arctic Circle	22-1

List of Tables

Table 1-1.	Composition of a Dry Earth's Atmosphere	1-1
Table 1-2.	Selected Properties of the Standard Atmosphere	1-6
Table 2-1.	Celsius Temperature Conversion Formulae	2-2
Table 2-2.	Fahrenheit Temperature Conversion Formulae	2-2
Table 2-3.	Heat (Thermal) Conductivity of Various Substances	2-7
Table 2-4.	Specific Heat Capacity of Various Substances	2-9
Table 3-1.	Latent Heat of Water at 0 °C	3-7
Table 5-1.	Units of Pressure	5-3
Table 5-2.	Pressure System Symbols	5-6
Table 5-3.	Common Constant Pressure Charts	5-9
Table 6-1.	Common Isopleths	6-2
Table 6-2.	Common Weather Chart Symbols	6-5
Table 11-1.	Air Parcel Vertical Motion Characteristics	11-4
Table 13-1.	Cloud Forms	13-1
Table 13-2.	Approximate Height of Cloud Bases above the Surface	13-2
Table 19-1.	Enhanced Fujita Scale (Enhanced F Scale) for Tornado Damage	19-11
Table 21-1.	Wind Speed and Characteristic House Damage for the Saffir-Simpson Hurricane Wind Scale	21-15

CHAPTER 1. THE EARTH'S ATMOSPHERE

1.1 **Introduction.** The Earth's atmosphere is a cloud of gas and suspended solids extending from the surface out many thousands of miles, becoming increasingly thinner with distance, but always held by the Earth's gravitational pull. The atmosphere is made up of layers surrounding the Earth that holds the air we breathe, protects us from outer space, and holds moisture (e.g., vapor, clouds, and precipitation), gases, and tiny particles. In short, the atmosphere is the protective bubble we live in.

This chapter covers our atmosphere's composition, vertical structure and the standard atmosphere.

1.2 **Composition.** The Earth's atmosphere consists of numerous gases (see Table 1-1) with the top four making up 99.998 percent of all gases. Nitrogen, by far the most common, dilutes oxygen and prevents rapid burning at the Earth's surface. Living things need it to make proteins. Oxygen is used by all living things and is essential for respiration. Plants use carbon dioxide to make oxygen. Carbon dioxide also acts as a blanket and prevents the escape of heat to outer space.

Table 1-1. Composition of a Dry Earth's Atmosphere

Gas	Symbol	Content (by Volume)
Nitrogen	N_2	78.084%
Oxygen	O_2	20.947%
Argon	Ar	0.934%
Carbon Dioxide	CO_2	0.033%
Neon	Ne	18.20 parts per million
Helium	He	5.20 parts per million
Methane	CH_4	1.75 parts per million
Krypton	Kr	1.10 parts per million
Sulfur dioxide	SO_2	1.00 parts per million
Hydrogen	H_2	0.50 parts per million
Nitrous Oxide	N_2O	0.50 parts per million
Xenon	Xe	0.09 parts per million

Gas	Symbol	Content (by Volume)
Ozone	O_3	0.07 parts per million
Nitrogen dioxide	NO_2	0.02 parts per million
Iodine	I_2	0.01 parts per million
Carbon monoxide	CO	trace
Ammonia	NH_3	trace

Note: The atmosphere always contains some water vapor in amounts varying from trace to about four percent by volume. As water vapor content increases, the other gases decrease proportionately.

Weather, the state of the atmosphere at any given time and place, strongly influences our daily routine as well as our general life patterns. Virtually all of our activities are affected by weather, but, of all our endeavors, perhaps none more so than aviation.

1.2.1 Air Parcel. An air parcel is an imaginary volume of air to which any or all of the basic properties of atmospheric air may be assigned. A parcel is large enough to contain a very large number of molecules, but small enough so that the properties assigned to it are approximately uniform. It is not given precise numerical definition, but a cubic centimeter of air might fit well into most contexts where air parcels are discussed. In meteorology, an air parcel is used as a tool to describe certain atmospheric processes, and we will refer to air parcels throughout this document.

1.3 **Vertical Structure.** The Earth's atmosphere is subdivided into five concentric layers (see Figure 1-1) based on the vertical profile of average air temperature changes, chemical composition, movement, and density. Each of the five layers is topped by a pause, where the maximum changes in thermal characteristics, chemical composition, movement, and density occur.

1.3.1 Troposphere. The troposphere begins at the Earth's surface and extends up to about 11 kilometers (36,000 feet) high. This is where we live. As the gases in this layer decrease with height, the air becomes thinner. Therefore, the temperature in the troposphere also decreases with height. As you climb higher, the temperature drops from about 15 °C (59 °F) to -56.5 °C (-70 °F). Almost all weather occurs in this region.

The vertical depth of the troposphere varies due to temperature variations which are closely associated with latitude and season. It decreases from the Equator to the poles, and is higher during summer than in winter. At the Equator, it is around 18-20 kilometers (11-12 miles) high, at 50° N and 50° S latitude, 9 kilometers (5.6 miles), and at the poles, 6 kilometers (3.7 miles) high. The transition boundary between the troposphere and the layer above is called the tropopause. Both the tropopause and the troposphere are known as the lower atmosphere.

1.3.2 <u>Stratosphere</u>. The stratosphere extends from the tropopause up to 50 kilometers (31 miles) above the Earth's surface. This layer holds 19 percent of the atmosphere's gases, but very little water vapor.

Temperature increases with height as radiation is increasingly absorbed by oxygen molecules, leading to the formation of ozone. The temperature rises from an average -56.6 °C (-70 °F) at the tropopause to a maximum of about -3 °C (27 °F) at the stratopause due to this absorption of ultraviolet radiation. The increasing temperature also makes it a calm layer, with movements of the gases being slow.

Commercial aircraft often cruise in the lower stratosphere to avoid atmospheric turbulence and convection in the troposphere. Severe turbulence during the cruise phase of flight can be caused by the convective overshoot of thunderstorms from the troposphere below. The disadvantages of flying in the stratosphere can include increased fuel consumption due to warmer temperatures, increased levels of radiation, and increased concentration of ozone.

Figure 1-1. Vertical Structure of the Atmosphere

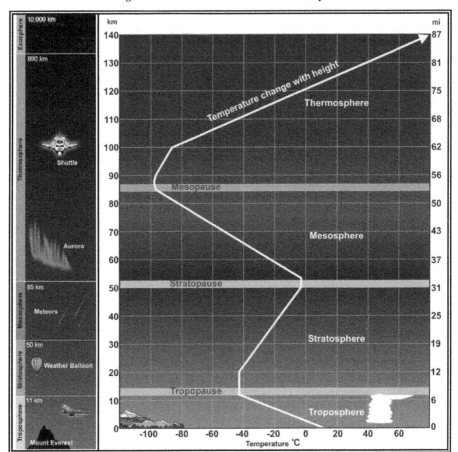

The regions of the stratosphere and the mesosphere, along with the stratopause and mesopause, are called the middle atmosphere. The transition boundary that separates the stratosphere from the mesosphere is called the stratopause.

1.3.3 Mesosphere. The mesosphere extends from the stratopause to about 85 kilometers (53 miles) above the Earth. The gases, including the number of oxygen molecules, continue to become thinner and thinner with height. As such, the effect of the warming by ultraviolet radiation also becomes less and less pronounced, leading to a decrease in temperature with height. On average, temperature decreases from about -3 °C (27 °F) to as low as -100 °C (-148 °F) at the mesopause. However, the gases in the mesosphere are thick enough to slow down meteorites hurtling into the atmosphere where they burn up, leaving fiery trails in the night sky.

1.3.4 Thermosphere. The thermosphere extends from the mesopause to 690 kilometers (430 miles) above the Earth. This layer is known as the upper atmosphere.

The gases of the thermosphere become increasingly thin compared to the mesosphere. As such, only the higher energy ultraviolet and x ray radiation from the sun is absorbed. But because of this absorption, the temperature increases with height and can reach as high as 2,000 °C (3,600 °F) near the top of this layer.

Despite the high temperature, this layer of the atmosphere would still feel very cold to our skin, because of the extremely thin air. The total amount of energy from the very few molecules in this layer is not sufficient enough to heat our skin.

1.3.5 Exosphere. The exosphere is the outermost layer of the atmosphere, and extends from the thermopause to 10,000 kilometers (6,200 miles) above the Earth. In this layer, atoms and molecules escape into space and satellites orbit the Earth. The transition boundary that separates the exosphere from the thermosphere is called the thermopause.

1.4 **The Standard Atmosphere.** Continuous fluctuations of atmospheric properties create problems for engineers and meteorologists who require a fixed standard for reference. To solve this problem, they defined a standard atmosphere, which represents an average of conditions throughout the atmosphere for all latitudes, seasons, and altitudes.

Standard atmosphere is a hypothetical vertical distribution of atmospheric temperature, pressure, and density that, by international agreement, is taken to be representative of the atmosphere for purposes of pressure altimeter calibrations, aircraft performance calculations, aircraft and missile design, ballistic tables, etc. (see Table 1-2 and Figure 1-2). Weather-related processes are generally referenced to the standard atmosphere, as are examples in this document.

Table 1-2. Selected Properties of the Standard Atmosphere

Property	Metric Units	English Units
Sea level pressure	1013.25 hectopascals	29.92 inches of mercury
Sea level temperature	15 °C	59 °F
Lapse rate of temperature in the troposphere	6.5 °C/1,000 meters	3.57 °F/1,000 feet
Pressure altitude of the tropopause	11,000 meters	36,089 feet
Temperature at the tropopause	-56.5 °C	-69.7 °F
Note: 1 hectopascal = 1 millibar.		

Figure 1-2. U.S. Standard Atmosphere within the Troposphere

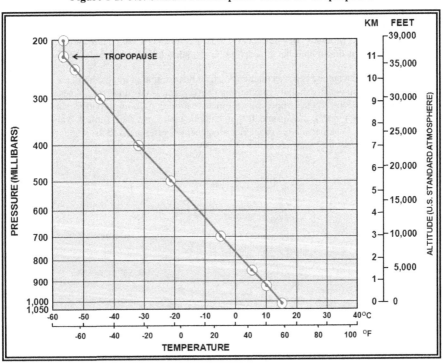

8/23/16

AC 00-6B

CHAPTER 2. HEAT AND TEMPERATURE

2.1 **Introduction.** Temperature is one of the most basic variables used to describe the state of the atmosphere. We know that air temperature varies with time from one season to the next, between day and night, and even from one hour to the next. Air temperature also varies from one location to another, from high altitudes and latitudes to low altitudes and latitudes. Temperature can be critical to some flight operations. As a foundation for the study of temperature effects on aviation and weather, this chapter describes temperature, temperature measurement, and heat transfer and imbalances.

2.2 **Matter.** Matter is the substance of which all physical objects are composed. Matter is composed of atoms and molecules, both of which occupy space and have mass. The Earth's gravity acting on the mass of matter produces weight.

2.3 **Energy.** Energy is the ability to do work. It can exist in many forms and can be converted from one form to another. For example, if a ball is located at the edge of a slide, it contains some amount of potential energy (energy of position). This potential energy is converted to kinetic energy (energy of motion) when the ball rolls down the slide. Atoms and molecules produce kinetic energy because they are in constant motion. Higher speeds of motion indicate higher levels of kinetic energy.

2.4 **Heat.** Heat is the total kinetic energy of the atoms and molecules composing a substance. The atoms and molecules in a substance do not all move at the same velocity. Thus, there is actually a range of kinetic energy among the atoms and molecules.

2.5 **Temperature.** Temperature is a numerical value representing the average kinetic energy of the atoms and molecules within matter. Temperature depends directly on the energy of molecular motion. Higher (warmer) temperatures indicate a higher average kinetic energy of molecular motion due to faster molecular speeds. Lower (colder) temperatures indicate a lower average kinetic energy of molecular motion due to slower molecular speeds. Temperature is an indicator of the internal energy of air.

2.5.1 Temperature Measurement. A thermometer is an instrument used to measure temperature. Higher temperatures correspond to higher molecular energies, while lower temperatures correspond to lower molecular energies.

2.5.2 Temperature Scales. Many scientists use the Kelvin (K) scale, which is a thermodynamic (absolute) temperature scale, where absolute zero, the theoretical absence of all thermal energy, is zero Kelvin (0 K). Thus, the Kelvin scale is a direct measure of the average kinetic molecular activity. Because nothing can be colder than absolute zero, the Kelvin scale contains no negative numbers.

The Celsius (°C) scale is the most commonly used temperature scale worldwide and in meteorology. The scale is approximately based on the freezing point (0 °C) and boiling point of water (100 °C) under a pressure of one standard atmosphere (approximately sea level). Each degree on the Celsius scale is exactly the same size as a degree on the Kelvin scale.

Table 2-1. Celsius Temperature Conversion Formulae

	From Celsius	To Celsius
Fahrenheit	[°F] = ([°C] x 9/5) + 32	[°C] = ([°F] − 32) x 5/9
Kelvin	[K] = [°C] + 273.15	[°C] = [K] − 273.15
For temperature *intervals* rather than specific temperatures, 1 °C = 274.15 K and 1 °C = 33.8 °F	

The United States uses Fahrenheit (°F) scale for everyday temperature measurements. In this scale, the freezing point of water is 32 degrees Fahrenheit (32 °F) and the boiling point is 212 degrees Fahrenheit (212 °F).

Table 2-2. Fahrenheit Temperature Conversion Formulae

	From Fahrenheit	To Fahrenheit
Celsius	[°C] = ([°F] − 32) x 5/9	[°F] = ([°C] x 9/5) + 32
Kelvin	[K] = ([°F] + 459.67) x 5/9	[°F] = ([K] x 9/5) − 459.67
For temperature *intervals* rather than specific temperatures, 1 °F = 255.93 K and 1 °F = -17.22 °C	

Figure 2-1. Comparison of Kelvin, Celsius, and Fahrenheit Temperature Scales

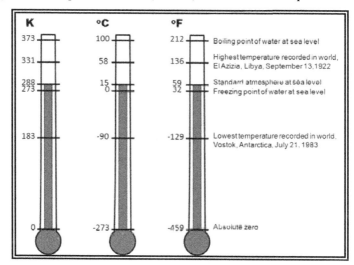

A thermometer changes readings due to the addition or subtraction of heat. Heat and temperature are not the same, but they are related.

2.6 **Heat Transfer.** Heat transfer is energy transfer as a consequence of temperature difference. When a physical body (e.g., an object or fluid) is at a different temperature than its surroundings or another body, transfer of thermal energy, also known as heat transfer (or heat exchange) occurs in such a way that the body and the surroundings reach thermal equilibrium (balance). Heat transfer always occurs from a hot body to a cold body. Where there is a temperature difference between objects in proximity, heat transfer between them can never be stopped; it can only be slowed down.

The heat source for the surface of our planet is the sun. Energy from the sun is transferred through space and through the Earth's atmosphere to the Earth's surface. Since this energy warms the surface and atmosphere, some of it becomes heat energy. There are three ways heat is transferred into and through the atmosphere: radiation, conduction, convection, or any combination of these. Heat transfer associated with the heat change of water from one phase to another (i.e., liquid water releases heat when changed to a vapor, liquid water absorbs heat when it changes to ice) can be fundamentally treated as a variation of convective heat transfer. The heat transfer associated with water will be discussed later.

2.6.1 <u>Radiation</u>. If you have stood in front of a fireplace or near a campfire, you have felt the heat transfer known as radiation. The side of your body nearest the fire warms, while your other side remains unaffected by the heat. Although you are surrounded by air, the air has nothing to do with this type of heat transfer. Heat lamps that keep food warm work in the same way.

Radiation is the transfer of heat energy through space by electromagnetic radiation. These electromagnetic waves travel at the speed of light and are usually described in terms of wavelength or frequency. Frequencies range from gamma rays on the high end to radio waves on the low end. Also contained in the spectrum are x ray, ultraviolet, visible, infrared, and microwave.

Figure 2-2. Radiation Example

All objects emit (radiate) energy as the heat energy within the object is converted to radiation energy. This transmitted radiation passes through entities such as air, water, or space. Along the way, the radiation can be reflected, which occurs when the wave energy changes direction when encountering an object. Eventually, the radiation is absorbed and the electromagnetic wave energy is converted to heat energy by the absorbing object. The emitting object loses heat energy, and the absorbing object gains heat energy during this process.

2.6.1.1 **Solar and Terrestrial Radiation.** All objects emit radiation energy, including the sun (solar radiation) and the Earth (terrestrial radiation). An object's wavelength of maximum radiation is inversely related to its temperature; the hotter (colder) the object, the shorter (longer) the wavelength. The sun's wavelength of maximum radiation is relatively short and is centered in the visible spectrum. The Earth's wavelength of maximum radiation is relatively long and is centered in the infrared spectrum.

Figure 2-3. Temperature's Effect on Radiation Wavelength

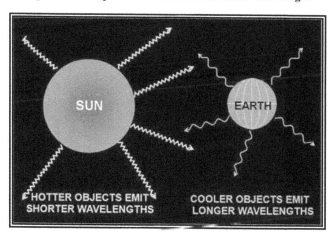

Some of the solar radiation that reaches the Earth's surface is radiated back into the atmosphere to become heat energy. Dark-colored objects such as asphalt absorb more of the radiant energy and warm faster than light-colored objects. Dark objects also radiate their energy faster than light-colored objects.

2.6.1.2 **Solar Zenith Angle.** The intensity of incoming solar radiation that strikes the Earth's surface (insolation) varies with solar zenith angle. Solar zenith angle is the angle measured from the Earth's surface between the sun and the zenith (i.e., directly overhead). Solar zenith angle varies with latitude, season, and the diurnal cycle (sunrise/sunset).

Figure 2-4 illustrates the concept. Insolation is maximized when the solar zenith angle is zero degrees (0°), which means the sun is directly overhead. With increasing solar zenith angle, the insolation is spread over an increasingly larger surface area (y is greater than x) so that the insolation becomes less intense. Also, with increasing solar zenith angle, the sun's rays must pass through more of the Earth's atmosphere, where they can be scattered and absorbed before reaching the Earth's surface. Thus, the sun can heat the surface to a much higher temperature when it is high in the sky, rather than low on the horizon.

Figure 2-4. Solar Zenith Angle

2.6.2 Conduction. Conduction is the transfer of energy (including heat) by molecular activity from one substance to another in contact, or through, a substance. Heat always flows from the warmer substance to the colder substance. The rate of heat transfer is greater with larger temperature differences and depends directly on the ability of the substance(s) to conduct heat. During conduction, the warmer substance cools and loses heat energy, while the cooler substance warms and gains heat energy.

Heat (thermal) conductivity is the property of a substance that indicates its ability to conduct heat as a consequence of molecular motion. Units are Watts per meter-Kelvin (W m^{-1} K^{-1}). Table 2-3 below provides the heat (thermal) conductivity of various substances. Note that air is a poor thermal conductor.

Table 2-3. Heat (Thermal) Conductivity of Various Substances

Material	Phase	Heat (Thermal) Conductivity (W m^{-1} K^{-1})
Silver	Solid	429
Copper	Solid	401
Aluminum	Solid	250
Iron	Solid	80
Sand (saturated)	Solid	2.7
Water (ice)	Solid (0 °C)	2.18
Sandstone	Solid	1.7
Limestone	Solid	1.26 – 1.33
Glass	Solid	1.05
Water (liquid)	Liquid	0.58
Sand (dry)	Solid	0.35
Soil	Solid	0.17 – 1.13
Wood (oak)	Solid	0.17
Wood (balsa)	Solid	0.055
Snow	Solid (<0 °C)	0.05 – 0.25
Air	Gas	0.024
Water (steam)	Gas (125 °C)	0.016

All measurements are at 25 °C unless otherwise noted.
Note: 1 K equals -272.15 °C.

2.6.3 <u>Convection</u>. Convection is the transport of heat within a fluid, such as air or water, via motions of the fluid itself. This type of heat flow takes place in liquids and gases because they can move freely, and it is possible to set up currents within them. Water boiling in a pot is an example of convection. Because air is a poor thermal conductor, convection plays a vital role in the Earth's atmospheric heat transfer process. Figure 2-5 illustrates examples of various heat transfer processes.

Figure 2-5. Heat Transfer Examples[1]

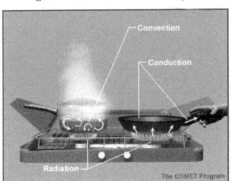

2.7　**Thermal Response.** Whether by radiation, conduction, convection, or a combination of these, the temperature response to the input (or output) of some specified quantity of heat varies from one substance to another. Specific heat capacity, also known simply as specific heat, is defined as the measure of heat energy required to increase the temperature of a unit quantity of a substance by a certain temperature interval. Specific heat capacity is typically expressed in units of joules per gram-Kelvin ($J\ g^{-1}\ K^{-1}$). Thus, two different substances with identical temperature measurements do not necessarily possess the same amount of heat energy. When exposed to the same amount of heat energy, a substance with a low specific heat capacity warms up more than a substance with a higher specific heat capacity.

---

[1] The source of this and other material labeled COMET® is the Web site at http://meted.ucar.edu/ of the University Corporation for Atmospheric Research (UCAR), sponsored in part through cooperative agreement(s) with the National Oceanic and Atmospheric Administration (NOAA), U.S. Department of Commerce (DOC). ©1997-2015 University Corporation for Atmospheric Research. All Rights Reserved.

Table 2-4. Specific Heat Capacity of Various Substances

Substance	Phase	Specific Heat Capacity ($J\ g^{-1}\ K^{-1}$)
Water (steam)	Gas (100 °C)	4.22
Water	Liquid (25 °C)	4.18
Wood (balsa)	Solid	2.90
Water (ice)	Solid (0 °C)	2.05
Wood (oak)	Solid	2.00
Soil (wet)	Solid	1.48
Sandy clay	Solid	1.38
Air (sea level, dry)	Gas	1.01
Asphalt	Solid	0.92
Clay	Solid	0.92
Aluminum	Solid	0.91
Brick (common)	Solid	0.90
Concrete	Solid	0.88
Glass	Solid	0.84
Limestone	Solid	0.84
Sand (quartz)	Solid	0.83
Soil (dry)	Solid	0.80
Granite	Solid	0.79
Iron	Solid	0.46
Copper	Solid	0.39
Mercury	Liquid	0.14
Lead	Solid	0.13

All measurements are at 25 °C unless otherwise noted.
Note: *1 K equals -272.15 °C.*

\Water has the highest specific heat capacity of any naturally occurring substance. That means it has a much higher capacity for storing heat energy than other substances, such as soil, sand, rock, or air. Water can store large amounts of heat energy while only experiencing a small temperature change.

Figure 2-6 below compares the specific heat capacity of water and sand. The specific heat capacity of water is more than five times that of quartz sand. Thus, 4.18 joules of heat are required to raise the temperature of one gram of water by 1 °C, while only 0.83 joules are required to raise the temperature of one gram of quartz sand by 1 °C. This is one reason why beach sand is hotter than water on a sunny, summer afternoon.

Figure 2-6. Specific Heat Capacity: Water Versus Sand

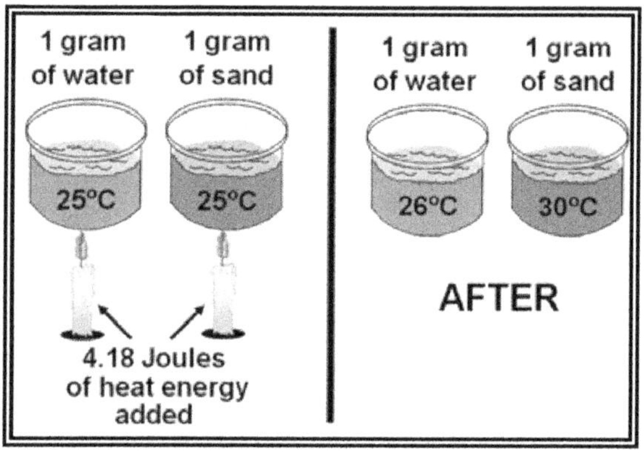

The difference in specific heat capacities is one of the primary reasons why the temperature of a body of water, such as a lake or the ocean, is less variable with time than the surface temperature of land. Water heats up more slowly than land during the day and during summer, and cools down more slowly at night and during the winter. Thus, a body of water exhibits greater resistance to temperature change, called thermal inertia, than does a land mass.

Heat flow differences are another reason why water bodies warm up and cool down more slowly than land. Incoming solar radiation penetrates water to significant depths, but can only heat the top skin layer of soil and rock. Also, since water is a fluid, its heat energy can be circulated through great volumes and depths via convection. Water temperature changes occur to depths of six meters (20 feet) or more on a daily basis, and 200 to 600 meters (650 to 1950 feet) annually. The process is more problematic over land since heat must be transferred via the slow process of conduction. Land temperature changes occur to depths of only 10 centimeters (4 inches) on a daily basis and 15 meters (50 feet) or less annually.

Water is much more resistant to temperature changes than land. It warms up and cools down more slowly than land and helps to moderate nearby air temperature. This is why islands and localities located immediately downwind from the ocean or a large lake (maritime locations) exhibit smaller diurnal and seasonal temperature variations than localities well inland (continental locations). Figure 2-7 illustrates this effect. Although both cities are at approximately the same latitude, the temperature is much less variable at San Francisco (maritime) than Kansas City (continental).

Figure 2-7. Variation of Mean Daily Temperatures for San Francisco (Maritime) and Kansas City (Continental)

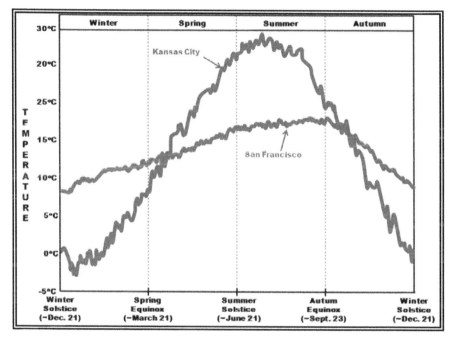

2.8   **Temperature Variations with Altitude.** A lapse rate of temperature is defined as a decrease in temperature with height. In Table 1-2, it was stated that the temperature decreases 6.5 °C/kilometer (3.57 °F/1,000 feet) in the standard atmosphere. But since this is an average, the exact value seldom exists. In fact, temperature in the troposphere sometimes remains constant or even increases with height. Caution should be taken when using the standard lapse rate to estimate the freezing level. Quite often the boundary layer is dry adiabatic and the estimate of freezing level could be in error.

2.8.1 Atmospheric Sounding. An atmospheric sounding, or simply sounding, is a plot of the vertical profile of one or more atmospheric parameters, such as temperature, dewpoint, or wind above a fixed location. Soundings are used extensively by meteorologists to determine the state of the atmosphere.

2.8.2 Isothermal Layer. An isothermal layer is a layer within the atmosphere where the temperature remains constant with height (see Figure 2-8).

Figure 2-8. Sounding with an Isothermal Layer

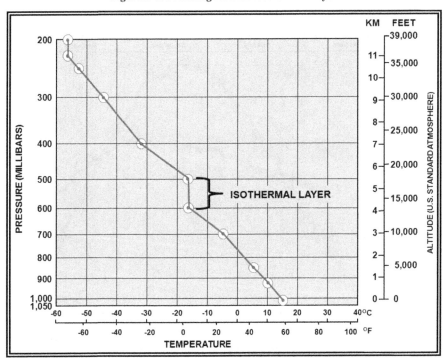

2.8.3 Temperature Inversion. A temperature inversion, or simply inversion, is a layer in which the temperature increases with altitude. If the base of the inversion is at the surface, it is termed a surface-based inversion. If the base of the inversion is not at the surface, it is termed an inversion aloft (see Figure 2-9).

A surface-based inversion typically develops over land on clear nights when wind is light. The ground radiates and cools much faster than the overlying air. Air in contact with the ground becomes cool, while the temperature a few hundred feet above changes very little. Thus, temperature increases with height.

An inversion may also occur at any altitude when conditions are favorable. For example, a current of warm air aloft overrunning cold air near the surface produces an inversion aloft. Inversions are common in the stratosphere.

The principal characteristic of an inversion layer is its marked stability, so that very little turbulence can occur within it. Turbulence will be discussed at length in Chapter 17.

Figure 2-9. Sounding with a Temperature Inversion

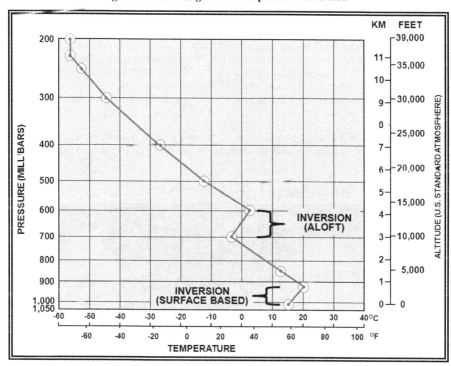

CHAPTER 3. WATER VAPOR

3.1 Introduction. Water vapor is the gaseous form of water and one of the most important of all constituents of the atmosphere. It constitutes only a small percentage of the Earth's atmosphere, varying from only trace amounts to 4 percent by volume, and its amount varies widely in space and time. Approximately half of all of the atmospheric water vapor is found below 2 kilometers (6,500 feet) altitude, and only a minute fraction of the total occurs above the tropopause.

Water vapor is important, not only as the raw material for clouds and precipitation (e.g., rain and snow), but also as a vehicle for the transfer of heat energy and as a regulator of the Earth's temperatures through absorption and emission of radiation, most significantly in the thermal infrared (i.e., the greenhouse effect). The amount of water vapor present in a given air sample may be measured in a number of different ways, involving such concepts as relative humidity and dewpoint. Before we talk about these subjects, we will first discuss how water cycles through the Earth-atmosphere system.

3.2 The Hydrologic Cycle. The hydrologic cycle (see Figure 3-1) involves the continuous circulation of water in the Earth-atmosphere system. Water vapor plays a critical role in the cycle.

Figure 3-1. The Hydrologic Cycle

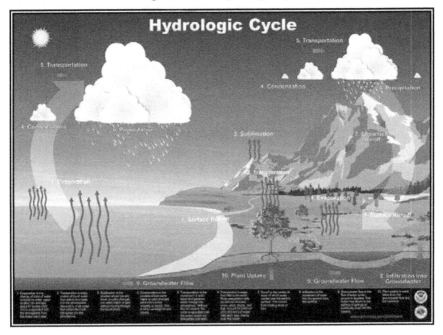

3.2.1 Evaporation. Evaporation is the phase transition by which a liquid is changed to a vapor (gas). In meteorology, the substance we are concerned about the most is water, and the primary source is the ocean. On average, about 120 centimeters (47 inches) is evaporated into the atmosphere from the ocean each year. For evaporation to take place, energy is required. The energy can come from any source: the sun, the atmosphere, the Earth, or objects on the Earth, such as humans.

Everyone has experienced evaporation personally. When the body heats up due to the air temperature, or through exercise, the body sweats, secreting water onto the skin. The purpose is to cause the body to use its heat to evaporate the liquid, thereby removing heat and cooling the body. The same effect can be seen when you step out of a shower or swimming pool. The coolness you feel is from the removal of bodily heat used to evaporate the water on your skin.

3.2.2 Transpiration. Transpiration is the evaporation of water from plants. In most plants, transpiration is a passive process largely controlled by the humidity of the atmosphere and the moisture content of the soil. Of the transpired water passing through a plant, only 1 percent is used in the growth process of the plant. The remaining 99 percent is passed into the atmosphere.

3.2.3 Sublimation. Sublimation is the phase transition by which a solid is changed into vapor (a gas) without passing through the liquid phase. In the atmosphere, sublimation of water occurs when ice and snow (solids) change into water vapor (a gas).

3.2.4 Condensation. Condensation is the phase transition by which vapor (a gas) is changed into a liquid. In the atmosphere, condensation may appear as clouds, fog, mist, dew, or frost, depending upon the physical conditions of the atmosphere.

3.2.5 Transportation. Transportation is the movement of solid, liquid, and gaseous water through the atmosphere. Without this movement, the water evaporated over the ocean would not precipitate over land.

3.2.6 Precipitation. Precipitation results when tiny condensation particles grow through collision and coalescence.

3.2.7 Runoff. Runoff occurs when there is excessive precipitation and the ground is saturated (i.e., cannot absorb any more water). This runoff flows into streams and rivers and eventually back into the sea.

Evaporation of this runoff into the atmosphere begins the hydrologic cycle over again. Some of the water percolates into the soil and into the ground water, only to be drawn into plants again for transpiration to take place.

3.2.8 Infiltration. Infiltration is the movement of water into the ground from the surface.

3.2.9 Groundwater Flow. Groundwater flow is the flow of water underground in aquifers. The water may return to the surface in springs or eventually seep into the oceans.

3.2.10 Plant Uptake. Plant uptake is water taken from the groundwater flow and soil moisture.

3.3 **Saturation.** Saturation is the maximum possible quantity of water vapor that an air parcel can hold at any given temperature and pressure. The term saturated air means an air parcel has all the water vapor it can hold, while unsaturated air means an air parcel can hold more water vapor.

3.4 **Relative Humidity.** Relative humidity is the ratio, usually expressed as a percentage, of water vapor actually in the air parcel compared to the amount of water vapor the air parcel could hold at a particular temperature and pressure.

$$Relative\ Humidity = \frac{Water\ vapor\ content}{Water\ vapor\ capacity}$$

While relative humidity is the most common method of describing atmospheric moisture, it is also the most misunderstood. Relative humidity can be confusing because it does not indicate the actual water vapor content of the air, but rather how close the air is to saturation. An air parcel with 100 percent relative humidity is saturated, while an air parcel with relative humidity less than 100 percent is unsaturated.

An air parcel's capacity to hold water vapor (at a constant pressure) is directly related to its temperature. It is possible to change an air parcel's relative humidity without changing its water vapor content. Figure 3-2 illustrates the concept below. An air parcel at sea level at a temperature of 30 °C has the capacity to hold 27 grams of water vapor. If it actually held 8 grams, its relative humidity would be 30 percent, and it would be unsaturated. However, if the air parcel's temperature decreases to 20 °C, its water vapor storage capacity decreases to 15 grams and its relative humidity rises to 53 percent. At 10 °C, the air parcel's water vapor storage capacity decreases to equal the amount of water vapor it actually holds (8 grams), its relative humidity increases to 100 percent, and it becomes saturated. During this cooling process, the air parcel's actual water vapor content remained constant, but relative humidity increased with decreasing temperature.

Figure 3-2. Temperature Effects on Relative Humidity

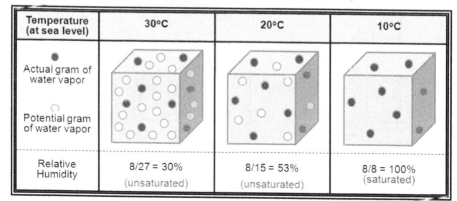

3.5 **Dewpoint.** Dewpoint is the temperature an air parcel must be cooled at constant pressure and constant water vapor pressure to allow the water vapor in the parcel to condense into water (dew). When this temperature is below 0 °C (32 °F), it is sometimes called the frost point. Lowering an air parcel's temperature reduces its capacity to hold water vapor.

3.6 **Temperature-Dewpoint Spread (Dewpoint Depression).** The difference between an air parcel's temperature and its dewpoint is the dewpoint depression, or commonly referred to as the spread. Surface aviation weather reports (e.g., Aviation Routine Weather Reports (METAR)/Aviation Selected Special Weather Reports (SPECI)) provide observations of both temperature and dewpoint. The temperature greatly affects the air parcel's ability to hold water vapor, while the dewpoint indicates the actual quantity of water vapor in the parcel. As the spread decreases, relative humidity increases. When the spread decreases to zero, relative humidity is 100 percent, and the air parcel is saturated. Figure 3-3 below illustrates the relationship between temperature-dewpoint spread and relative humidity.

Surface temperature-dewpoint spread is important in anticipating fog, but has little bearing on precipitation. To support precipitation, air must be saturated through thick layers aloft.

Figure 3-3. Temperature-Dewpoint Spread Effect on Relative Humidity

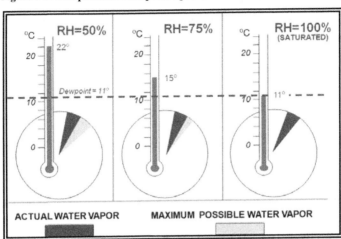

Relative humidity (RH) depends on the temperature-dewpoint spread. In Figure 3-3, dewpoint is constant but temperature decreases from left to right. On the left panel, relative humidity is 50 percent, which indicates the air parcel could hold twice as much water vapor as is actually present. As the air parcel cools, the temperature-dewpoint spread decreases while relative humidity increases. When the air parcel's temperature cools to equal its dewpoint (11 °C), its capacity to hold water vapor is reduced to the amount actually present. The temperature-dewpoint spread is zero, relative humidity is 100 percent, and the air parcel is now saturated.

3.7 Change of Phase. Water changes from one state of matter (solid, liquid, or vapor) to another at the temperatures and pressures experienced near the surface of the Earth. Interestingly, water is the only substance on Earth that exists naturally in all three phases: as water droplets and ice crystals (visible as clouds) and as water vapor.

Water has some unique thermal properties which make it a powerful heat transport mechanism. It has the highest specific heat capacity of any naturally occurring substance (see Table 2-4). That means water has a much higher capacity for storing heat energy (with little resulting temperature change) than other substances. These properties make water an ideal heat transport mechanism, and have important implications on weather and climate.

3.7.1 Latent Heat. Latent heat is the quantity of heat energy either released or absorbed by a unit mass of a substance when it undergoes a phase transition (change of state). Units are typically expressed in terms of joules per gram (J/g). Figure 3-4 below illustrates the latent heat transactions that occur when water undergoes phase transition.

Figure 3-4. Latent Heat Transactions when Water Undergoes Phase Transition

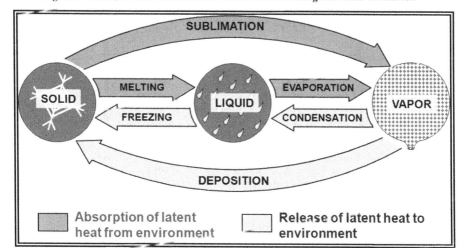

Heat is exchanged between water and its environment during phase transition. Although the temperature of the environment changes in response, the temperature of the water undergoing the phase transition remains constant until the phase change is complete; that is, the available heat, latent heat, is involved exclusively in changing the phase of water and not in changing its temperature. There are six phase transitions, three of which are associated with the absorption of latent heat by water from the environment (melting, evaporation, and sublimation), and three of which are associated with the release of heat energy by water to the environment (freezing, condensation, and deposition).

Melting is the phase transition by which a solid is changed to a liquid. During melting, water absorbs 334 joules per gram due to the latent heat of fusion. Freezing, the reverse process, releases 334 joules per gram back to the environment.

Evaporation is the phase transition by which a liquid is changed to a vapor. During evaporation, water absorbs 2,501 joules per gram due to the latent heat of vaporization. Condensation, the reverse process, releases 2,501 Joules per gram back to the environment.

Sublimation is the phase transition by which a solid is changed to a vapor. During sublimation, water absorbs 2,834 joules per gram due to the latent heat of sublimation. Deposition, the reverse process, releases 2,834 joules per gram back to the environment.

Table 3-1. Latent Heat of Water at 0 °C

Latent Heat Type	Energy Exchange (J/g)
Latent heat of sublimation	2,834
Latent heat of vaporization	2,501
Latent heat of fusion	334

The amount of energy associated with latent heat exchange should not be understated. An average hurricane releases 52 million trillion (5.2 x 10^{19}) joules per day as water vapor condenses into clouds and precipitation. This is equivalent to about 40 times the total worldwide energy consumption per day in 2005!

CHAPTER 4. EARTH-ATMOSPHERE HEAT IMBALANCES

4.1   Introduction. Weather is not a capricious act of nature, but rather the atmosphere's response to unequal rates of radiational heating and cooling across the surface of the Earth and within its atmosphere. The absorption of incoming solar radiation causes heating, while the emission of outgoing terrestrial radiation causes cooling. However, imbalances in the rate of heating and cooling create temperature gradients.[2] Atmospheric circulations and weather are the atmosphere's never-ending attempt to redistribute this heat and achieve equilibrium.

4.2   The Earth-Atmosphere Energy Balance. The Earth-atmosphere energy balance is the balance between incoming energy from the sun (solar radiation) and outgoing energy from the Earth (terrestrial radiation), as seen in Figure 4-1. When solar radiation reaches the Earth, some is reflected back to space by air (8 percent), clouds (17 percent), or the surface (6 percent). Some is absorbed by water vapor/dust/ozone (19 percent) or by clouds (4 percent). The remainder is absorbed by the Earth's surface (46 percent).

Figure 4-1. Earth-Atmosphere Energy Balance

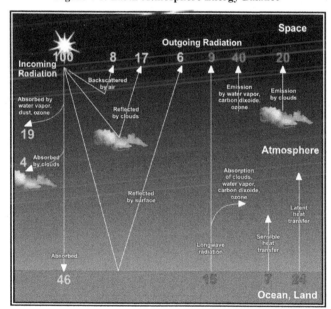

100 units of incoming radiation from the sun is balanced by 100 units of outgoing radiation from the Earth.

---

[2] A gradient describes the rate of change of a feature (in this case temperature) per unit of distance.

However, since the Earth is much cooler than the sun, its radiating energy is much weaker (long wavelength) infrared energy. We can indirectly see this energy radiate into the atmosphere as heat (e.g., rising from a hot road, creating shimmers on hot sunny days). The Earth-atmosphere energy balance is achieved as the energy received from the sun (solar radiation) balances the energy lost by the Earth back into space (terrestrial radiation). In this way, the Earth maintains a stable average temperature.

The absorption of infrared radiation trying to escape from the Earth back to space is particularly important to the global energy balance. Energy absorption by the atmosphere stores more energy near its surface than it would if there was no atmosphere. The average surface temperature of the moon, which has no atmosphere, is -18 °C (0 °F). By contrast, the average surface temperature of the Earth is 15 °C (59 °F). This heating effect is called the greenhouse effect.

Greenhouse warming is enhanced during nights when the sky is overcast (see Figure 4-2). Heat energy from the Earth can be trapped by clouds, leading to higher temperatures as compared to nights with clear skies. The air is not allowed to cool as much with overcast skies. Under partly cloudy skies, some heat is allowed to escape, and some remains trapped. Clear skies allow for the most cooling to take place.

Figure 4-2. Greenhouse Effect on Nighttime Radiational Cooling

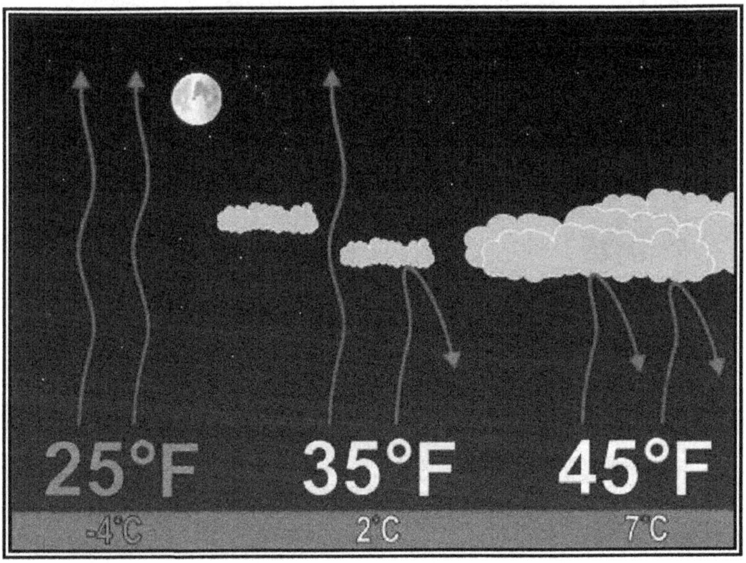

25°F -4°C
35°F 2°C
45°F 7°C

4.3 Heat Imbalances Between Earth's Surface and the Atmosphere.

The Earth-atmosphere energy balance numbers (see Figure 4-1) indicate that both sensible heat (7 percent) and latent heat (24 percent) processes transfer heat from the Earth's surface into its atmosphere. Both processes are necessary to prevent the Earth's surface from continually heating up and the atmosphere from continually cooling down.

4.3.1 Sensible Heating.
Sensible heating involves both conduction and convection. It occurs due to differences in air density. Warm air is less dense than cool air.

On warm sunny days, the Earth's surface is heated by incoming solar radiation or insolation. However, the heating is somewhat uneven because certain areas of the Earth's surface absorb more heat from the sun than others. Heat is conducted from the relatively warm ground to the cooler overlying air, which warms a shallow layer of air near the ground. The heated air expands, becomes less dense than the surrounding cooler air, and rises. Through this process, a large bubble of warm air called a thermal rises and transfers heat energy upwards (see Figure 4-3). Cooler, denser air sinks toward the ground to replace the rising air. This cooler air becomes heated in turn, rises, and repeats the cycle.

Figure 4-3. Development of a Thermal

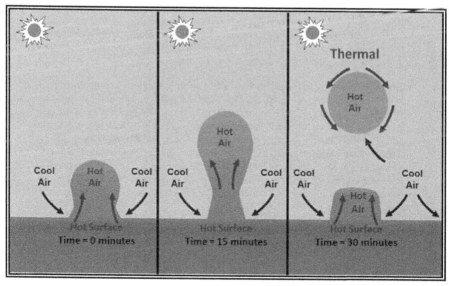

In this manner, convection transports heat from the Earth's surface into the atmosphere. Because air is a poor conductor of heat (see Table 2-3), convection is much more important than conduction as a heat transport mechanism within the atmosphere.

Figure 4-4. Example of Convection in the Atmosphere

4.3.2 <u>Latent Heat</u>. The phase transition of water and associated latent heat exchanges (see subparagraph 3.7.1) are largely responsible for transferring the excess heat from the surface of the Earth into its atmosphere. As the Earth's surface absorbs radiation, some of the heat produced is used to evaporate (vaporize) water from oceans, lakes, rivers, soil, and vegetation. The water absorbs heat energy due to the latent heat of vaporization. Some of this water vapor condenses to microscopic water droplets or deposits as ice crystals that are visible as clouds. During cloud formation, the water vapor changes state, and latent heat is released into the atmosphere. During this process, the excess heat is transferred from the Earth's surface into its atmosphere.

4.4 **Heat Imbalance Variations with Latitude.** Global imbalances in radiational heating and cooling occur not only vertically between the Earth's surface and its atmosphere, but also horizontally with latitude. Since the Earth is essentially spherical, parallel beams of incoming solar radiation strike lower latitudes more directly than higher latitudes (see Figure 4-5); that is, the solar zenith angle is lower, and the sun is more directly overhead in equatorial regions than at the poles. At higher latitudes, solar radiation is spread over a larger area and is less intense per unit surface area than at lower latitudes. Thus, the Earth absorbs more solar radiation at lower latitudes than higher latitudes, which creates heat imbalances and temperature gradients between the Equator and the poles.

Figure 4-5. Solar Zenith Angle Variations with Latitude

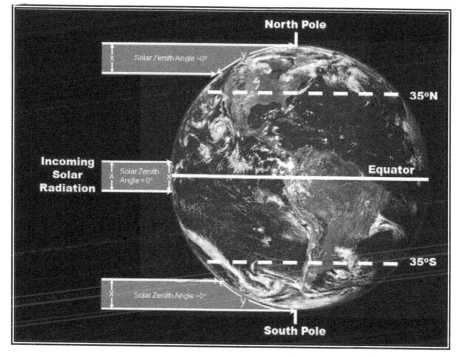

The emission of terrestrial radiation also varies by latitude, but less so than the absorption of solar radiation. Terrestrial radiation emission decreases with increasing latitude due to a drop in temperature with latitude. Thus, at higher latitudes, the annual rate of cooling exceeds the rate of warming, while the reverse is true at lower latitudes.

Averaged over all latitudes, incoming solar radiation must equal outgoing terrestrial radiation. Otherwise, the Earth would be unable to maintain a constant average temperature. About 35° latitude in both hemispheres is where incoming and outgoing radiation is equal. This implies there is annual net cooling at higher latitudes and net warming at lower latitudes. However, we know this is untrue. The excess heat in the tropics must be transported polar by some mechanism(s). This poleward heat transport is accomplished by atmospheric circulations, weather, and ocean currents.

4.5 Seasons. Seasons are caused by the tilt of the Earth's rotational axis as the Earth orbits the sun (see Figure 4-6). The Earth's rotational axis is tilted by 23½° from the perpendicular drawn to the plane of the Earth's orbit about the sun and points the same direction in space all year long. The North Pole is tilted most directly toward the sun Solstice (~December 22). Thus, in the Northern Hemisphere, the longest day of the year (lowest solar zenith angle) occurs on the Summer Solstice, while the shortest day of the year (highest solar zenith angle) occurs on the Winter Solstice. Day and night are of equal length (12 hours) worldwide on the Vernal Equinox (~March 21) and the Autumnal Equinox (~September 23).

Figure 4-6. Solar Zenith Angle Variations with Northern Hemisphere Seasons

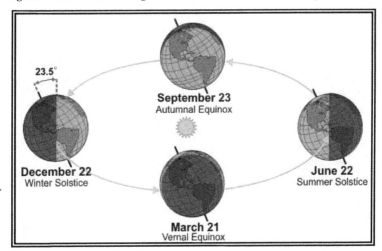

Figure 4-7 illustrates the average seasonal temperature variation in the Northern Hemisphere for both maritime and continental locations. Note that the warmest (coldest days) of the year occur after the summer (winter) solstice. This is due to the time lag necessary for heat flow processes to fully heat (cool) the surface of the Earth.

Figure 4-7. Average Seasonal Temperature Variation in the Northern Hemisphere

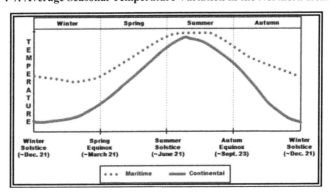

4.6   Diurnal Temperature Variation. Diurnal temperature variation is the daytime maximum and nighttime minimum of air temperature due to variations of insolation caused by the rising and setting of the sun (variations of solar zenith angle) as the Earth rotates around its axis. Figure 4-8 depicts the typical diurnal temperature and radiation variations over land when the sky is clear.

Figure 4-8. Clear Sky Diurnal Temperature and Radiation Variations Over Land

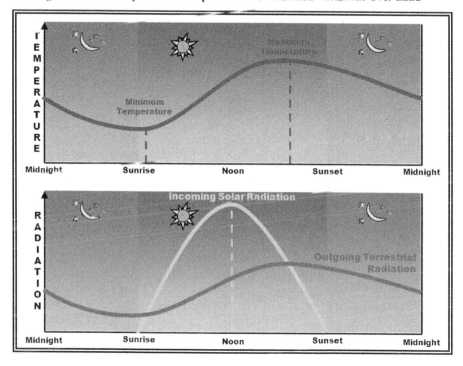

Warming and cooling of the Earth depend on an imbalance between solar and terrestrial radiation. The Earth receives heat during the day through incoming solar radiation. It loses heat to space by outgoing terrestrial radiation both day and night.

Shortly after sunrise, incoming solar radiation received at the Earth's surface (insolation) becomes greater than outgoing terrestrial radiation and the Earth's surface warms. Peak isolation occurs around noon, but maximum surface air temperature usually occurs during the midafternoon. This lag is necessary for the air near the ground to heat up due to conduction and convection with the surface. The Earth begins to cool once the rate of outgoing terrestrial radiation exceeds the rate of insolation.

At night, insolation is absent, but outgoing terrestrial radiation continues and the Earth's surface continues to cool. Cooling continues until shortly after sunrise, when incoming solar radiation once again exceeds outgoing terrestrial radiation. Minimum surface air temperature usually occurs shortly after sunrise.

The magnitude of diurnal temperature variation is primarily influenced by surface type, latitude, sky cover (e.g., clouds or pollutants), water vapor content of the air, and wind speed. Temperature variation is maximized over land, at low latitudes, with a clear sky, dry air, and light wind. Conversely, temperature variation is minimized over water, at high latitudes, with a cloudy sky, moist air, and strong wind.

CHAPTER 5. ATMOSPHERIC PRESSURE AND ALTIMETRY

5.1 Introduction. Atmospheric pressure is one of the most basic variables used to describe the state of the atmosphere and is commonly reported in weather observations. Unlike temperature and relative humidity, changes in atmospheric pressure are not as readily sensed by people. However, variations of pressure across the Earth are associated with pressure centers (either high pressure centers or low pressure centers) that cause the wind to blow and can bring important weather changes. Density, which is directly related to pressure, is a property of the atmosphere which can be used by pilots to help determine how their aircraft will perform at various altitudes.

This chapter discusses atmospheric pressure, how it is measured, and how it varies across the Earth. This chapter also covers the altimeter, which is a pressure sensor used by pilots to determine altitude. Finally, density will be discussed, along with its relationship to density altitude.

5.2 Atmospheric Pressure. The atoms and molecules that make up the various layers in the atmosphere are always moving in random directions. Despite their tiny size, when they strike a surface they exert pressure.

Each molecule is too small to feel and only exerts a tiny bit of pressure. However, when we add up all the pressures from the large number of molecules that strike a surface each moment, the total pressure is considerable. This is air pressure. As the density of the air increases, then the number of strikes per unit of time and area also increases.

Since molecules move in all directions, they even exert air pressure upwards as they smash into objects from underneath. Air pressure is exerted in all directions.

Atmospheric pressure is the force per unit area exerted by the weight of the atmosphere. Since air is not solid, we cannot weigh it with conventional scales. Yet, three centuries ago, Evangelista Torricelli proved he could weigh the atmosphere by balancing it against a column of mercury. He actually measured pressure converting it directly to weight.

Figure 5-1. Air Has Weight

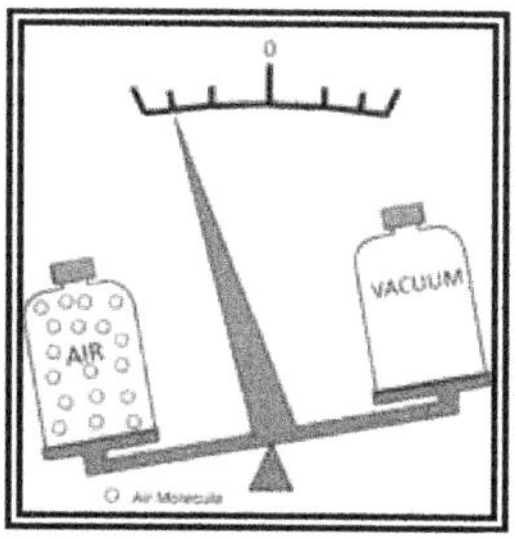

Air is composed of matter and, thus, has weight due to the pull of Earth's gravity.

5.2.1 Barometer. The instrument Torricelli designed to measure pressure was called a barometer. The aneroid barometer is the type mostly commonly used by meteorologists and the aviation community.

Essential features of an aneroid barometer (see Figure 5-2) are a flexible metal cell and the registering mechanism. Air is taken out of the cell to create a partial vacuum. The cell contracts or expands as pressure changes. One end of the cell is fixed, while the other end moves the registering mechanism. The coupling mechanism magnifies the movement of the cell driving an indicator hand along a scale graduated in pressure unit.

Figure 5-2. Aneroid Barometer

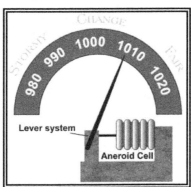

5.2.2 Atmospheric Pressure Units. Atmospheric pressure is expressed in many ways throughout the world (see Table 5-1). Meteorologists worldwide have long measured atmospheric pressure in millibars (mb or mbar), which denote pressure as a force per square centimeter. However, after the introduction of the International System of Units (SI) in 1960, the hectopascal (hPa) was adopted by most countries and is used in the Aviation Routine Weather Report (METAR)/Aviation Selected Special Weather Report (SPECI) code first developed in 1968. Many meteorologists prefer to use the term they learned during their education and work experience. Therefore, some continue to use the term millibars, while others use hectopascals (which are equivalent). The unit inch of mercury (inHg or Hg) is still used in the United States for altimetry.

Table 5-1. Units of Pressure

Units of Pressure	Standard Atmosphere Value at Sea Level	Common Use
Hectopascals (hPa)	1013.2 hPa	METAR/SPECI
Millibars (mb or mbar)	1013.2 mb	U.S. Weather Charts
Inches of mercury (inHg or Hg)	29.92 inHg	U.S. Aviation
Pounds per square inch (psi)	14.7 psi	U.S. Engineering

5.2.3   Station Pressure. The pressure measured at an airport is called station pressure, or the actual pressure at field elevation. Pressure is lower at higher altitudes. Therefore, airports with higher field elevations usually have lower pressure than airports with lower field elevations. For instance, station pressure at Denver is less than at New Orleans (see Figure 5-3).

Figure 5-3. Station Pressure

Station Pressure Denver 24.92"

Station Pressure New Orleans 29.92"

The next few subparagraphs will examine some factors that influence pressure.

5.2.4   Pressure Variation. Atmospheric pressure varies with altitude and the temperature of the air, as well as with other minor influences, such as water vapor.

5.2.4.1   Pressure Changes with Altitude. As we move upward through the atmosphere, the weight of the air above us decreases. If we carry a barometer with us, we can measure a decrease in pressure as the weight of the air above us decreases. Figure 5-4 shows the pressure decrease with height in the standard atmosphere.

Figure 5-4. Air Pressure in the Standard Atmosphere

(millibars)	(feet) / meters
100	53,000 / 16,200 m
200	39,000 / 11,800 m
300	30,000 / 9,200 m
400	24,000 / 7,200 m
500	18,000 / 5,600 m
600	14,000 / 4,200 m
700	10,000 / 3,000 m
1000	300

Mt. Denali, AK 20,320 ft.

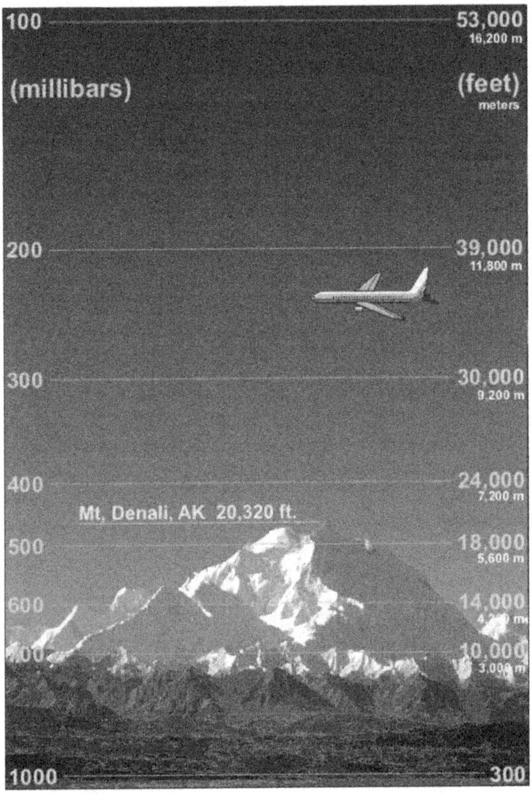

These standard altitudes are based on standard temperatures. In the real atmosphere, temperatures are seldom standard, so we will explore temperature effects on pressure in the following subparagraphs.

5.2.4.2   Temperature Effects on Pressure. Like most substances, air expands as it becomes warmer and contracts as it cools. Figure 5-5 shows three columns of air: one colder than standard, one with standard temperature, and one warmer than standard. Pressure is equal at the bottom and top of each column. Vertical expansion of the warm column has made it taller than the

5-4

column at standard temperature. Contraction of the cold column has made it shorter than the standard column. Since the total pressure decrease is the same in each column, the rate of decrease of pressure with height in warm air is less than standard, while the rate of decrease in pressure with height in cold air is greater than standard.

Figure 5-5. Temperature Effect on Pressure

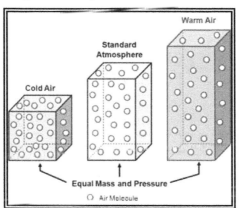

5.2.5 <u>Sea Level Pressure</u>. Since pressure varies greatly with altitude, we cannot readily compare station pressures between stations at different altitudes. To make them comparable, we adjust them to some common level. Mean sea level (MSL) is the most useful common reference. In Figure 5-6 pressure measured at a station at a 5,000-foot elevation is 25 inches; pressure increases about 1 inch of mercury for each 1,000 feet, or a total of 5 inches. Sea level pressure is approximately 25 + 5, or 30 inches of mercury.

Figure 5-6. Reduction of Station Pressure to Sea Level

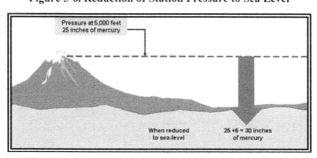

Sea level pressure is typically displayed on surface weather charts. Pressure continually changes across the Earth, so a sequence of surface charts must be viewed to follow these changing pressures.

5.2.5.1 Sea Level Pressure Analyses (Surface Chart). After plotting sea level pressure on a surface chart, lines are drawn connecting points of equal sea level pressure. These lines of equal pressure are isobars. Hence, the surface chart is an isobaric analysis showing identifiable, organized pressure patterns. Four pressure systems are commonly identified: low, high, trough and ridge (see Table 5-2 and Figure 5-7).

Table 5-2. Pressure System Symbols

Pressure System	Symbol	Definition
Low	L	A minimum of atmospheric pressure in two dimensions (closed isobars) on a surface chart, or a minimum of height (closed contours) on a constant pressure chart. Also known as a cyclone.
High	H	A maximum of atmospheric pressure in two dimensions (closed isobars) on a surface chart, or a maximum of height (closed contours) on a constant pressure chart. Also known as an anticyclone.
Trough	╲ ╲	An elongated area of relatively low atmospheric pressure.
Ridge	∧∧∧	An elongated area of relatively high atmospheric pressure.

Figure 5-7. Surface Chart Pressure Patterns

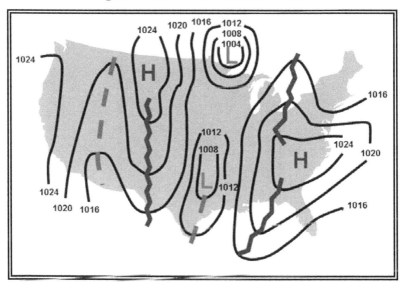

5.2.6 Constant Pressure Surface. A constant pressure surface is a surface along which the atmospheric pressure is everywhere equal at a given instant. For instance, the 500 millibar constant pressure surface has a pressure of 500 millibars everywhere on it. The height (altitude) of a constant pressure surface varies primarily due to temperature; these heights can be measured by a rawinsonde.

    5.2.6.1 Rawinsonde Observations. The National Weather Service (NWS) takes routine scheduled upper air observations, usually referred to as soundings. A balloon carries a rawinsonde instrument (see Figure 5-8), which consists of radio gear and sensing elements. While in flight, the rawinsonde transmits pressure, temperature, and relative humidity data. Wind speed and direction aloft are obtained by tracking the position of the radiosonde in flight using Global Positioning Satellites (GPS). Most stations around the world take rawinsonde observations. However, meteorologists and other data users frequently refer to a rawinsonde observation as a radiosonde observation.

Figure 5-8. Weather Balloon and Radiosonde

5.2.6.2 **Constant Pressure Surface Analysis (Upper Air Chart).** These heights measured by the rawinsonde (and other types of instruments) are plotted on a constant pressure chart and analyzed by drawing a line connecting points of equal height. These lines are called height contours. What is a height contour?

First, consider a topographic map with contours showing variations in elevation. These are height contours of the terrain surface. The Earth's surface is a fixed reference, and variations in its height are contoured.

The same concept applies to height contours on an upper air chart, except the reference is a constant pressure surface. Varying heights of the pressure surface are contoured. For example, a 700 millibar constant pressure analysis is a contour map of the heights of the 700 millibar pressure surface. While the contour map is based on variations in height, these variations are small when compared to flight levels, and for all practical purposes, one may regard the 700 millibar chart as a weather chart at approximately 3,000 meters (10,000 feet) above MSL.

A contour analysis (see Figure 5-9) shows highs, ridges, lows, and troughs aloft just as the isobaric analysis shows such systems at the surface. These systems of highs/ridges and lows/troughs are called pressure waves. These pressure waves are very similar to waves seen on bodies of water. They have crests (ridges) and valleys (troughs) and are in constant movement.

Figure 5-9. 500 Millibar Constant Pressure Chart

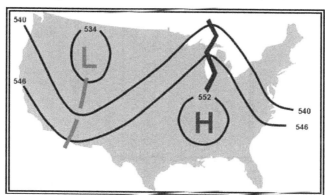

Table 5-3. Common Constant Pressure Charts

Chart	Pressure Altitude (approximate)	
	Feet (ft)	Meters (m)
100 mb	53,000 ft	16,000 m
150 mb	45,000 ft	13,500 m
200 mb	39,000 ft	12,000 m
250 mb	34,000 ft	10,500 m
300 mb	30,000 ft	9,000 m
500 mb	18,000 ft	5,500 m
700 mb	10,000 ft	3,000 m
850 mb	5,000 ft	1,500 m
925 mb	2,500 ft	750 m

5.3 **Density.** Density is the ratio of any quantity to the volume or area it occupies. Atmospheric density is defined as ratio of the mass (or weight) of the air to the volume occupied by it, usually expressed in kilograms per cubic meter (see Figure 5-10).

Figure 5-10. Density is Mass (Weight) per Volume

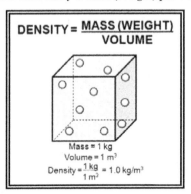

5.3.1 Volume Effects on Density. The density of an air parcel varies inversely with its volume. Assuming equal mass, an air parcel with a higher density has a smaller volume than an air parcel with a lower density (see Figure 5-11).

Figure 5-11. Volume Effects on Density

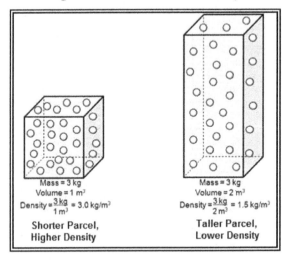

The shorter parcel (that is, the parcel with the smaller volume) has a higher density than the taller parcel which contains the larger volume. This is due to the fact that the air molecules within the shorter parcel must be compressed within the smaller volume.

5.3.2 Changes in Density. In general, the density of an air parcel can be changed by changing its mass, pressure, or temperature. Boyle's law says that the density of an ideal gas (ρ, the Greek letter rho) is given by:

$$\rho = \frac{MP}{RT}$$

Where M is the molar mass, P is the pressure, R is the universal gas constant, and T is the absolute temperature.

5.3.3 Density Effects on Pressure. Density is directly related to pressure. Assuming constant mass and temperature, an air parcel with a higher pressure is denser than an air parcel with a lower pressure.

As we have already seen, air pressure decreases with height in the atmosphere. Therefore, the density also decreases with height (see Figure 5-12). In the atmosphere, pressure has the greatest effect on density in the vertical direction.

Figure 5-12. Pressure Effects on Density in the Atmosphere

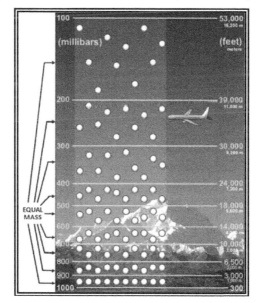

5.3.4 Temperature Effects on Density. Density is inversely related to temperature. Assuming constant mass and pressure, an air parcel with a higher temperature is less dense than an air parcel with a lower temperature (see Figure 5-13). This is because the warmer air occupies a large volume.

Figure 5-13. Temperature Effects on Density

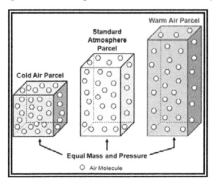

In the atmosphere, temperature has the most effect on density in the horizontal direction; that is, with horizontal changes of location (e.g., New York City versus Miami), temperature has the greatest effect on density.

5.3.5 Water Vapor Effects on Density. Density of an air parcel is inversely related to its quantity of water vapor. Assuming constant pressure, temperature, and volume, air with a greater amount of water vapor is less dense than air with a lesser amount of water vapor. This is because dry air molecules have a larger mass (weight) than water vapor molecules, and density is directly related to mass (see Figure 5-14).

Figure 5-14. Water Vapor Effects on Density

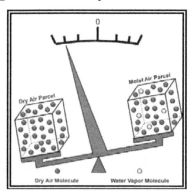

5.4 **Altimetry.** The altimeter is essentially an aneroid barometer. The difference is the scale. The altimeter is graduated to read increments of altitude rather than units of pressure. The standard for graduating the altimeter is the standard atmosphere.

5.4.1 Altitude. Altitude seems like a simple term: it means the vertical elevation of an object above the surface of the Earth. But in aviation, it can have many meanings.

    5.4.1.1 **True Altitude.** Since existing conditions in a real atmosphere are seldom standard, altitude indications on the altimeter are seldom actual or true altitudes. True altitude is the actual vertical distance above MSL.
If an altimeter does not indicate true altitude, what does it indicate?

    5.4.1.2 **Indicated Altitude.** Figure 5-13 shows the effect of mean temperature on the thickness of three columns of air. Pressures are equal at the bottoms and tops of the three layers. Since an altimeter is essentially an aneroid barometer, altitude indicated by the altimeter at the top of each column would be the same. To see this effect more clearly, see Figure 5-15. In the warm air column, a pilot would fly at an altitude that is higher than the indicated altitude. In the cold air column, the pilot would fly at an altitude lower than the indicated altitude.

Figure 5-15. True Versus Indicated Altitude

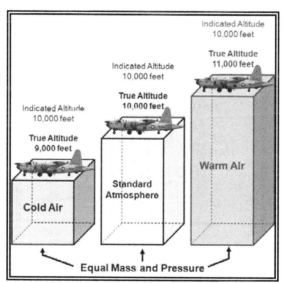

Height indicated on the altimeter also changes with changes in surface pressure. A movable scale on the altimeter permits the pilot to adjust for surface pressure, but he or she has no means of adjusting the altimeter for mean temperature of the column of air below. Indicated altitude is the altitude above MSL indicated on the altimeter when set at the local altimeter setting. But what is altimeter setting?

5.4.1.2.1 Altimeter Setting. Since the altitude scale is adjustable, a pilot can set his or her altimeter to read true altitude at some specified height. Takeoff and landing are the most critical phases of flight; therefore, airport elevation is the most desirable altitude for a true reading of the altimeter. The altimeter setting is the value to which the scale of the pressure altimeter is set so the altimeter indicates true altitude at field elevation.

To ensure the altimeter reading is compatible with altimeter readings of other aircraft in the vicinity, a pilot must ensure the altimeter setting is current. He or she must adjust it frequently while in flight, according to the nearest surface weather reporting station. Figure 5-16 shows the trouble a pilot can encounter if not vigilant in adjusting the altimeter during flight. As he or she flies from high pressure to low pressure, the plane is lower than the altimeter indicates.

Figure 5-16. Pressure Change Effects on Altimeter Readings

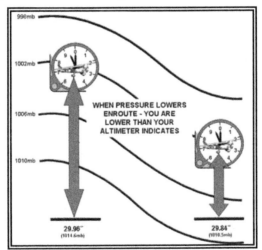

Figure 5-17. Temperature Change Effects on Altimeter Readings

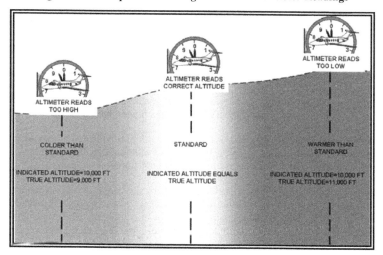

Figure 5-17 shows that as a pilot flies from warm to cold air, the altimeter reads too high—he or she is lower than the altimeter indicates. Over flat terrain, this lower-than-true reading is no great problem; other aircraft in the vicinity also are flying indicated rather than true altitude, and everyone's altimeter readings are compatible. If flying in cold weather over mountainous areas, however, a pilot must take this difference between indicated and true altitude into account. He or she must know that the true altitude assures clearance of terrain, and compute a correction to indicated altitude.

5.4.1.3 **Corrected (Approximately True) Altitude.** If a pilot could always determine mean temperature of a column of air between the aircraft and the surface, flight computers would be designed to use this mean temperature in computing true altitude. However, the only guide a pilot has to temperature below him is free air temperature at his altitude. Therefore, the flight computer uses outside air temperature to correct indicated altitude to approximate true altitude. The corrected (approximately true) altitude is indicated altitude corrected for the temperature of the air column below the aircraft, the correction being based on the estimated deviation of the existing temperature from standard atmosphere temperature. It is a close approximation to true altitude and is labeled true altitude on flight computers. It is close enough to true altitude to be used for terrain clearance, provided the pilot has his altimeter set to the value reported from a nearby reporting station.

5.4.1.4 **Pressure Altitude.** In the standard atmosphere, sea level pressure is 29.92 inches of mercury (1013.2 millibars). Pressure decreases at a fixed rate upward through the standard atmosphere. Therefore, in the standard atmosphere, a given pressure exists at any specified altitude. Pressure altitude is the altitude (above MSL) shown by the altimeter when set to 29.92 inches of mercury. In other words, it is the altitude associated with a specific pressure measured by the static port when the altimeter is set to 29.92. Since pressure is the same everywhere regardless of the specific pressure altitude, a constant pressure surface defines a constant pressure altitude. When a pilot flies a constant pressure altitude, he or she is flying a constant pressure surface.

As discussed earlier, constant pressure surfaces have different heights across them. Therefore, when flying at a specific pressure altitude (i.e., constant pressure surface) a pilot's true altitude will change with distance. However, since pressure altitudes are flown at or above FL180 (in the United States), a pilot will almost always be above the highest terrain features.

5.5 **Density Altitude.** Density altitude is the pressure altitude corrected for temperature deviations from the standard atmosphere. Density altitude bears the same relation to pressure altitude as true altitude does to indicated altitude.

Density altitude is indirectly related to atmospheric density; as air density increases (decreases), the density altitude decreases (increases). Airports with higher field elevations (e.g., Denver) have lower pressure, lower density, and, therefore, higher density altitudes than airports with lower field elevations (e.g., New Orleans).

Density altitude equals field elevation during standard atmospheric conditions, but conditions are rarely standard. Density altitude is higher (lower) than standard at airports that report lower (higher) than standard pressures (29.92 inches of mercury) and/or higher (lower) than standard temperatures. Temperature is the most important factor since temperature has the greatest effect on density horizontally in the atmosphere. On hot days, the air becomes less dense, causing high density altitudes. On cold days the air is denser, causing lower density altitudes. Dewpoint (water vapor) is also a contributing factor, but its effects are generally negligible.

Density altitude is an index to aircraft performance. Higher (lower) density altitude decreases (increases) performance. High density altitude is a hazard since it reduces aircraft performance in the following three ways:

1. It reduces power because the engine takes in less air to support combustion.
2. It reduces thrust because there is less air for the propeller to work with, or a jet has less mass of gases to force out of the exhaust.
3. It reduces lift because the light air exerts less force on the airfoils.

A pilot cannot detect the effect of high density altitude on his airspeed indicator. The aircraft lifts off, climbs, cruises, glides, and lands at the prescribed indicated airspeeds; but at a specified indicated airspeed, the pilot's true airspeed and groundspeed increase proportionally as density altitude becomes higher.

The net results are that high density altitude lengthens a pilot's takeoff, and landing rolls and reduces his or her rate of climb. Before lift-off, the plane must attain a faster groundspeed, and, therefore, needs more runway; and the reduced power and thrust add a need for still more runway. The plane lands at a faster groundspeed and, therefore, needs more room to stop. At a prescribed indicated airspeed, it is flying at a faster true airspeed, and, therefore, covers more distance in a given time, which means climbing at a shallower angle. Adding to this are the problems of reduced power and rate of climb. Figure 5-18 shows the effect of density altitude on takeoff distance and rate of climb.

Figure 5-18. High Density Altitude Effects on Flight

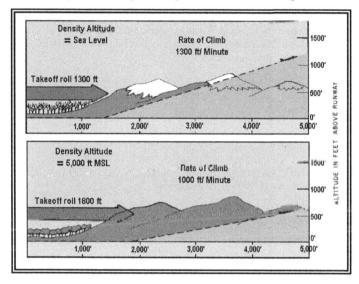

High density altitude also can be a problem at cruising altitude. When air temperature is higher (warmer) than standard atmosphere, the higher density altitude lowers the service ceiling. For example, if temperature at a pressure altitude of 10,000 feet is 20 °C, density altitude is 12,700 feet. A pilot's aircraft will perform as though it were at 12,700 feet indicated with a normal temperature of -8 °C.

To compute density altitude, a pilot can set the altimeter to 29.92 inches (1013.2 millibars), read the pressure altitude from the altimeter, obtain the outside air temperature, and then use a flight computer to compute density altitude.

CHAPTER 6. WEATHER CHARTS

6.1 **Introduction.** A weather chart is a map on which data and analyses are presented that describe the state of the atmosphere over a large area at a given moment in time.

The possible variety of such charts is enormous, but in meteorological history there has been a more or less standard set of charts, including surface charts and the constant pressure charts of the upper atmosphere. Because weather systems are three-dimensional (3-D), both surface and upper air charts are needed. Surface weather charts depict weather on a constant-altitude (usually sea level) surface, while upper air charts depict weather on constant-pressure surfaces.

The National Weather Service (NWS) produces many weather charts that support the aviation community. Refer to the current edition of AC 00-45, Aviation Weather Services, for details.

6.2 **Weather Observation Sources.** Weather analysis charts can be based on observations from a variety of data sources, including:

- Land surface (e.g., automated surface observing system (ASOS), Automated Weather Observing System (AWOS), and mesonet);
- Marine surface (e.g., ship, buoy, Coastal-Marine Automated Network (C-MAN), and tide gauge);
- Sounding (e.g., radiosonde, dropsonde, pibal, profiler, and Doppler weather radar Velocity Azimuth Display (VAD) wind profile);
- Aircraft (e.g., Aircraft Reports (AIREP), Pilot Weather Reports (PIREP), Aircraft Meteorological Data Relay (AMDAR), and Aircraft Communications Addressing and Reporting System (ACARS)); and
- Satellite.

Figure 6-1. Weather Observation Sources

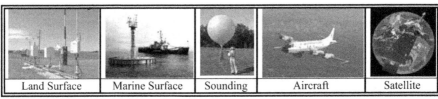

| Land Surface | Marine Surface | Sounding | Aircraft | Satellite |

6.3 **Analysis.** Analysis is the drawing and interpretation of the patterns of various elements on a weather chart. It is an essential part of the forecast process. If meteorologists do not know what is currently occurring, it is nearly impossible to predict what will happen in the future. Computers have been able to analyze weather charts for many years and are commonly used in the process. However, computers cannot interpret what they analyze. Thus, many meteorologists still perform a subjective analysis of weather charts when needed.

6.3.1 Analysis Procedure. The analysis procedure is similar to drawing in a dot-to-dot coloring book. Just as one would draw a line from one dot to the next, analyzing weather charts is similar in that lines of equal values, or isopleths, are drawn between dots representing various elements of the atmosphere. An isopleth is a broad term for any line on a weather map connecting points with equal values of a particular atmospheric variable.

Table 6-1. Common Isopleths

Isopleth	Variable	Definition
Isobar	Pressure	A line connecting points of equal or constant pressure.
Contour Line (also called isoheight)	Height	A line of constant elevation above MSL of a defined surface, typically a constant pressure surface.
Isotherm	Temperature	A line connecting points of equal or constant temperature.
Isotach	Wind Speed	A line connecting points of equal wind speed.
Isohume	Humidity	A line drawn through points of equal humidity.
Isodrosotherm	Dewpoint	A line connecting points of equal dewpoint.

The weather chart analysis procedure begins with a map of the plotted data which is to be analyzed (see Figure 6-2). It is assumed that bad or obviously incorrect data has been removed before beginning the analysis process. At first, the chart will appear to be a big jumble of numbers. But when the analysis procedure is complete, patterns will appear, and significant weather features will be revealed.

6.3.1.1 **Step 1: Determine the Optimal Contour Interval and Values to be Analyzed.** The first step in the weather chart analysis procedure is to identify the maxima and minima data values and their ranges to determine the optimal contour interval and values to be analyzed. The best contour interval will contain enough contours to identify significant weather features, but not so many that the chart becomes cluttered. Each weather element has a standard contour interval on NWS weather charts, but these values can be adjusted in other analyses as necessary.

8/23/16   AC 00-6B

Figure 6-2. Analysis Procedure Step 1: Determine the Optimal Contour Interval and Values to be Analyzed

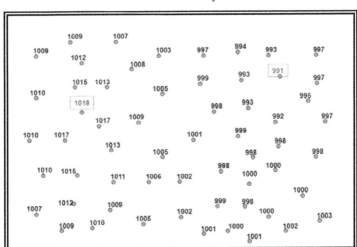

Every contour value must be evenly divisible by the contour interval. So, for example, if the contour interval is every 4 units, a 40-unit contour is all right, but a 41-unit contour is not. In the surface pressure analysis example shown in Figure 6-2, we will perform an isobar analysis beginning at a value of 992 millibars and use a contour interval of 4 millibars, which is standard on the NWS Surface Analysis Chart.

6.3.1.2   **Step 2: Draw the Isopleths and Extrema.** The second step is to draw the isopleths and extrema (maxima and minima) using the beginning contour value and contour interval chosen in the first step. It is usually easiest to begin drawing an isopleth either at the edge of the data domain (edge of the chart), or at a data point that matches the isopleth value being drawn. Interpolation must often be used to draw isopleths between data points and determine the extrema. Interpolate means to estimate a value within an interval between known values.

When drawing isopleths and extrema on a weather chart, certain rules must be followed:

- The analysis must remain within the data domain. Analysis must never be drawn beyond the edge of the chart where there are no data points. That would be guessing.

- Isopleths must not contain waves and kinks between two data points. This would indicate a feature too small to be supported by the data. Isopleths should be smooth and drawn generally parallel to each other.

6-3

- When an isopleth is complete, all data values must be higher than the isopleth's value on one side of the line and lower on the other.
- A closed loop isopleth must contain an embedded extremum (maximum or minimum).
- When a maximum (minimum) is identified, data values must decrease (increase) in all directions away from it.
- Isopleths can never overlap, intersect, or cross over extrema. It is impossible for one location to have more than one data value simultaneously.
- Each isopleth must be labeled. A label must be drawn wherever an isopleth exits the data domain. For closed loop isopleths, a break in the loop must be created where a label can be drawn. For very long and/or complex isopleths, breaks should be created where additional labels can be drawn, as necessary.
- Extrema must be labeled. Extrema are often denoted by an "x" embedded within a circle. Beneath the label, the analyzed value of the field must be written and underlined.
- Isopleths and labels should not be drawn over the data point values. If necessary, breaks in the isopleths should be created so that the data point values can still be read.

Figure 6-3. Analysis Procedure Step 2: Draw the Isopleths and Extrema

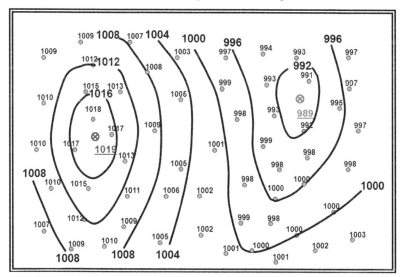

6.3.1.3　**Step 3: Identify Significant Weather Features.** The third (and final) step is to interpret significant weather features. The conventional labels for extrema are H (high) and L (low) for pressure and height, W (warm) and K (cold) for temperature (they stand for the German words for warm and cold), and X (maxima) and N (minima) for all other elements. Troughs, ridges, and other significant features are often identified as well. Table 6-2 below provides a list of the most common weather chart symbols. Refer to AC 00-45 for details on specific NWS weather charts.

Table 6-2. Common Weather Chart Symbols

Feature	Symbol	Definition
Low	L	A minimum of atmospheric pressure in two dimensions (closed isobars) on a surface chart, or a minimum of height (closed contours) on a constant pressure chart. Also known as a cyclone.
High	H	A maximum of atmospheric pressure in two dimensions (closed isobars) on a surface chart, or a maximum of height (closed contours) on a constant pressure chart. Also known as an anti-cyclone.
Trough	(dashed line)	An elongated area of relatively low atmospheric pressure or height.
Ridge	(zigzag line)	An elongated area of relatively high atmospheric pressure or height. May also be used as reference to other meteorological quantities, such as temperature and dewpoint.

In the surface pressure analysis below in Figure 6-4, a high, low, trough, and ridge have been identified.

Figure 6-4. Analysis Procedure Step 3: Interpret Significant Weather Features

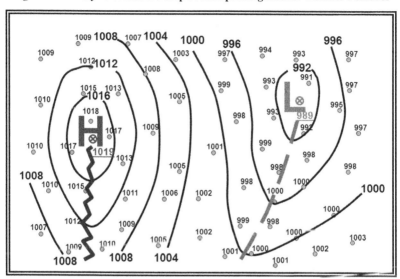

6.4 **Surface Chart.** A surface chart (also called surface map or sea level pressure chart) is an analyzed chart of surface weather observations. Essentially, a surface chart shows the distribution of sea level pressure, including the positions of highs, lows, ridges, and troughs, and the location and character of fronts and various boundaries, such as drylines, outflow boundaries, and sea breeze fronts. Although the pressure is referred to as MSL, all other elements on this chart are presented as they occur at the surface point of observation. A chart in this general form is the one commonly referred to as the weather map.

Figure 6-5. Example of a Surface Chart

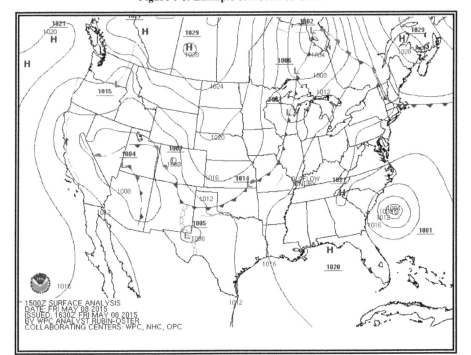

6.5   **Constant Pressure Chart.** A constant pressure chart (also called an isobaric chart) is a weather map representing conditions on a surface of equal atmospheric pressure. For example, a 500 millibar chart will display conditions at the level of the atmosphere at which the atmospheric pressure is 500 millibars. Constant pressure charts usually contain plotted data and analyses of the distribution of height of the surface (contours), wind (isotachs), temperature (isotherms), and sometimes humidity (isohumes). The height above sea level at which the pressure is that particular value may vary from one location to another at any given time, and also varies with time at any one location, so it does not represent a surface of constant altitude/height (i.e., the 500 millibar level may be at a different height above sea level over Dallas than over New York at a given time, and may also be at a different height over Dallas from one day to the next).

Constant pressure charts are most commonly known by their pressure value. For example, the 1,000 millibar chart (which closely corresponds to the surface chart), the 850 millibar chart, 700 millibar chart, 500 millibar chart, etc.

A contour analysis (see Figure 6-6) can reveal highs, ridges, lows, and troughs aloft just as the surface chart shows such systems at the surface. These systems of highs/ridges and lows/troughs are called pressure waves. These pressure waves are similar to waves seen on bodies of water. They have crests (ridges) and valleys (troughs).

Figure 6-6. Example of a 500 Millibar Constant Pressure Chart

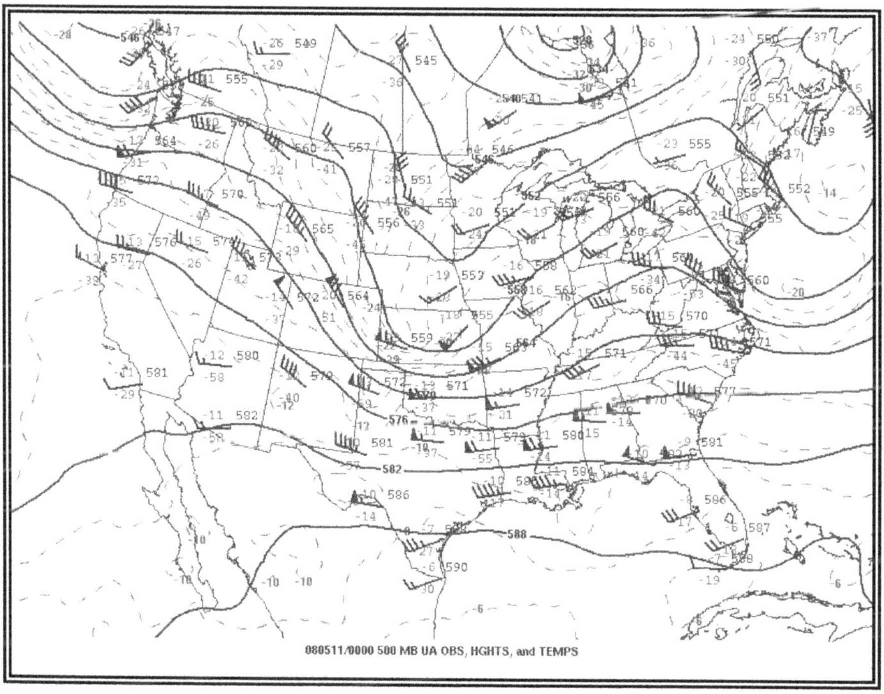

CHAPTER 7. WIND

7.1 **Introduction.** Wind is the air in motion relative to the surface of the Earth. Although we cannot actually see the air moving, we can measure its motion by the force that it applies on objects. For example, leaves rustling or trees swaying on a windy day indicate that the wind is blowing. Winds are a major factor to both weather and aircraft. Winds cause the formation, dissipation, and redistribution of weather. Winds also affect aircraft during all phases of flight. This chapter discusses how winds are named and the origin of wind.

7.2 **Naming of the Wind.** Wind is named according to the direction from which it is blowing. For example, a west wind indicates the wind is blowing from the west to the east. In aviation, 36 points of the compass are normally used to represent the direction from which the wind is blowing. For example, north winds come from 360°, east from 90°, south from 180°, and west from 270°.

7.3 **Forces That Affect the Wind.** Three primary forces affect the flow of wind: Pressure Gradient Force (PGF), Coriolis force, and friction.

7.3.1 <u>Pressure Gradient Force (PGF)</u>. Wind is driven by pressure differences which create a force called the Pressure Gradient Force (PGF). Whenever a pressure difference develops over an area, the PGF makes the wind blow in an attempt to equalize pressure differences. This force is identified by height contour gradients on constant pressure charts and by isobar gradients on surface charts.

PGF is directed from higher height/pressure to lower height/pressure and is perpendicular to contours/isobars. Whenever a pressure difference develops over an area, the PGF begins moving the air directly across the contours/isobars.

Figure 7-1. Direction of Pressure Gradient Force

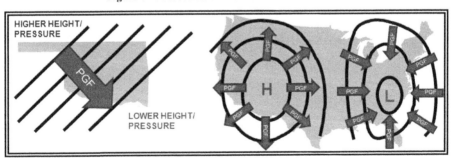

PGF is directed across contours/isobars towards lower height/pressure.

Wind speed is directly proportional to the PGF, which itself is directly proportional to the contour/isobar gradient. Closely spaced contours/isobars indicate strong winds, while widely spaced contours/isobars mean lighter wind. From a pressure analysis, you can get a general idea of wind speed from contour/isobar spacing.

Figure 7-2. Magnitude of Pressure Gradient Force

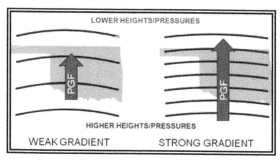

On the left panel, the contours/isobars are widely spaced apart, PGF is weak, and the wind speed is weak. On the right panel, the contours/isobars are more closely spaced, the PGF is stronger, and the wind speed is stronger.

The wind would flow from high to low pressure if the PGF was the only force acting on it. However, because of the Earth's rotation, there is a second force called the Coriolis force that affects the direction of wind flow.

7.3.2 Coriolis Force. A moving mass travels in a straight line until acted on by some outside force. However, if one views the moving mass from a rotating platform, the path of the moving mass relative to his platform appears to be deflected or curved. To illustrate, consider a turntable. If one used a pencil and a ruler to draw a straight line from the center to the outer edge of the turntable, the pencil will have traveled in a straight line. However, stopping the turntable, it is evident that the line spirals outward from the center (see Figure 7-3). To a viewer on the turntable, some apparent force deflected the pencil to the right.

Figure 7-3. Illustration of Coriolis Force

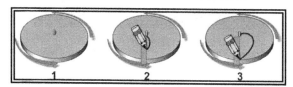

A similar apparent force deflects moving particles on the Earth. Because the Earth is spherical, the deflective force is much more complex than the simple turntable example. Although the force is termed apparent to us on Earth, it is very real. The principle was first explained by the Frenchman Gaspard-Gustave de Coriolis, and now carries his name—the Coriolis force.

Coriolis force affects all moving objects. The force deflects air to the right in the Northern Hemisphere and to the left in the Southern Hemisphere.

Coriolis force is at a right angle to wind direction and directly proportional to wind speed; that is, as wind speed increases, Coriolis force increases. At a given latitude, double the wind speed and you double the Coriolis force. Why at a given latitude?

Coriolis force varies with latitude from zero at the Equator to a maximum at the poles. It influences wind direction everywhere except immediately at the Equator, but the effects are more pronounced in middle and high latitudes.

Figure 7-4. Coriolis Force Variations Across the Earth

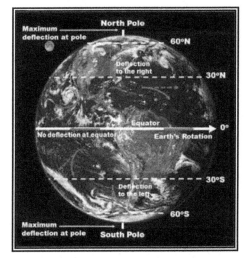

Coriolis force deflects moving objects to the right of their path in the Northern Hemisphere and to the left of their path in the Southern Hemisphere. Coriolis deflection is maximized at the poles and zero at the Equator.

Figure 7-5. Coriolis Force Magnitude Variations with Wind Speed

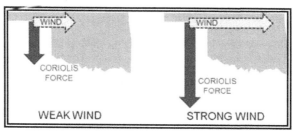

Coriolis force magnitude is directly proportional to wind speed. Wind speed is twice as strong in the right panel; thus, the Coriolis force is doubled.

7.3.3   Friction Force. Friction between the wind and the terrain surface slows the wind. The rougher the terrain, the greater the frictional effect. Also, the stronger the wind speed, the greater the friction. One may not think of friction as a force, but it is a very real and effective force always acting opposite to wind direction.

Figure 7-6. Friction Force Magnitude Variations with Terrain Roughness

Friction force magnitude is directly proportional to terrain roughness. Even though the wind speed is the same in both panels, the terrain is rougher in the right panel; thus, the friction force is stronger.

Figure 7-7. Friction Force Magnitude Variations with Wind Speed

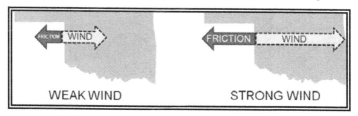

Friction force magnitude is directly proportional to wind speed. Wind speed is twice as strong in the right panel; thus, the friction force is doubled.

The frictional drag of the ground normally decreases with height and becomes insignificant above the lowest few thousand feet. However, this may vary somewhat since both strong winds and rough terrain extend the friction layer to higher altitudes.

7.4 Upper Air Wind. In the atmosphere above the friction layer (lowest few thousand feet), only PGF and Coriolis force affect the horizontal motion of air. Remember that the PGF drives the wind and is oriented perpendicular to height contours. When a PGF is first established, wind begins to blow from higher to lower heights directly across the contours. However, the instant air begins moving, Coriolis force deflects it to the right. Soon the wind is deflected a full 90° and is parallel to the contours. At this time, Coriolis force exactly balances PGF, as shown in Figure 7-8. With the forces in balance, wind will remain parallel to contours. This is called the geostrophic wind.

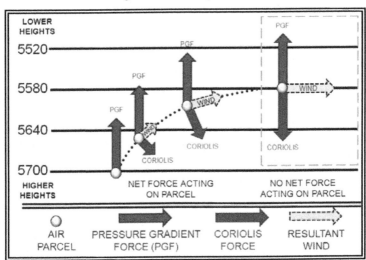

Figure 7-8. Geostrophic Wind

Figure 7-9. Upper Air Wind Flow

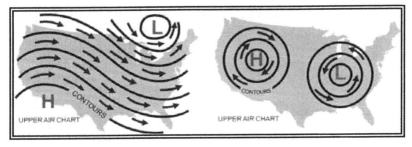

7.5 Surface Wind. At the surface of the Earth, all three forces come into play. As frictional force slows the wind speed, Coriolis force decreases. However, friction does not affect PGF. PGF and Coriolis force are no longer in balance. The stronger PGF turns the wind at an angle across the isobars toward lower pressure until the three forces balance, as shown in Figure 7-10.

Figure 7-10. Surface Wind Forces

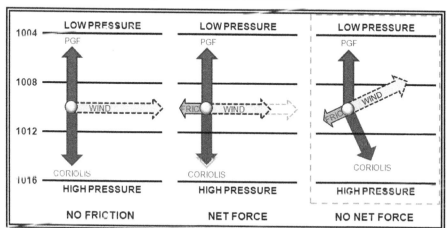

The angle of surface wind to isobars is about 10° over water, increasing to as high as 45° over rugged terrain. The end result is, in the Northern Hemisphere, the surface wind spirals clockwise and outward from high pressure, and counterclockwise and inward into low pressure (see Figure 7-11). In mountainous regions, one often has difficulty relating surface wind to pressure gradient because of immense friction, and also because of local terrain effects on pressure.

Figure 7-11. Surface Wind Flow

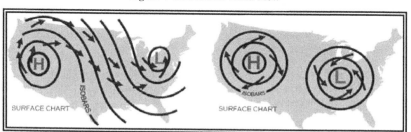

CHAPTER 8. GLOBAL CIRCULATIONS AND JET STREAMS

8.1 Non-Rotating Earth Circulation System. Global circulations explain how air and storm systems travel over the Earth's surface. The global circulation would be simple (and the weather boring) if the Earth did not rotate, the rotation was not tilted relative to the sun, and had no water.

Without those factors, the ground and atmosphere directly beneath the sun would be subject to more of the sun's heat than anywhere else on the planet. The result would be the Equator becoming very hot, with the hot air rising into the upper atmosphere.

That hot air would then move toward the poles, where it would become very cold and sink, returning to the Equator (see Figure 8-1). One large area of high pressure would be at each of the poles, with a large belt of low pressure around the Equator.

Figure 8-1. Non-Rotating, Non-Tilted, Waterless, Earth Circulation System

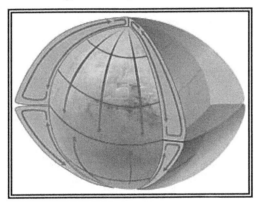

8.2 Rotating Earth Circulation System. However, since the Earth rotates, the axis is tilted, and there is more land mass in the Northern Hemisphere than in the Southern Hemisphere, the actual global pattern is much more complicated.

Instead of one large circulation between the poles and the Equator, there are three circulations (see Figure 8-2):

- Hadley cell—Low-latitude air movement toward the Equator that, with heating, rises vertically with poleward movement in the upper atmosphere. This forms a convection cell that dominates tropical and subtropical climates.

- Ferrel cell—A mid-latitude mean atmospheric circulation cell for weather named by William Ferrel in the 19th century. In this cell, the air flows poleward and eastward near the surface, and equatorward and westward at higher levels.

- Polar cell—Air rises, diverges, and travels toward the poles. Once over the poles, the air sinks, forming the polar highs. At the surface, air diverges outward from the polar highs. Surface winds in the polar cell are easterly (polar easterlies).

Figure 8-2. Earth Circulation System

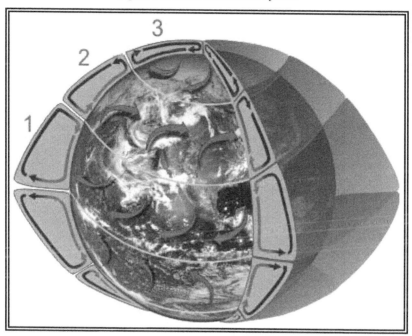

Between each of these circulation cells are bands of high and low pressure at the surface. The high pressure band is located about 30° N/S latitude and at each pole. Low pressure bands are found at the Equator and 50°-60° N/S.

Usually, fair and dry/hot weather is associated with high pressure, with rainy and stormy weather associated with low pressure. The results of these circulations become evident on a globe. Consider the number of deserts located along the 30° N/S latitude around the world compared to the region between 50°-60° N/S latitude. The higher latitudes, especially near the west coast of continents, tend to have more precipitation due to more storms moving around the Earth at these latitudes.

8.3 Jet Streams.

8.3.1 Introduction. Jet streams are relatively narrow bands of strong wind in the upper levels of the atmosphere. The winds blow from west to east in jet streams, but the flow often meanders southward and northward in waves. Jet streams follow the boundaries between hot and cold air. Since these hot and cold air boundaries are most pronounced in winter, jet streams are the strongest for both the Northern and Southern Hemisphere winters.

8.3.2 Direction of Wind Flow. Why do the jet stream winds blow from west to east? As stated in the previous section, if the Earth was not rotating, the warm air would rise at the Equator and move toward both the poles. The Earth's rotation divides this circulation into three cells. Likewise, the Earth's rotation is responsible for the jet stream.

The motion of the air is not directly north and south, but rather is affected by the momentum the air has as it moves away from the Equator and how fast a location on or above the Earth moves relative to the Earth's axis.

An object's speed relative to the Earth's axis depends on its location. Someone standing on the Equator is moving much faster than someone standing on a 45° latitude line. In Figure 8-3, the person at the position on the Equator arrives at the yellow line sooner than the other two. Someone standing on a pole is not moving at all (except that he or she would be slowly spinning). The speed of the rotation is great enough to cause a person to weigh one pound less at the Equator than he or she would at the North or South Pole.

Figure 8-3. Speed Relative to the Earth's Axis Versus Latitude

The momentum of air as it travels around the Earth is conserved, which means as the air that is over the Equator starts moving toward one of the poles, it keeps its eastward motion constant. The Earth below the air, however, moves slower, as that air travels toward the poles. The result is that the air moves faster and faster in an easterly direction (relative to the Earth's surface below) the farther it moves from the Equator.

8.3.3 Location. In addition, with the three cell circulations mentioned previously, the regions around 30° N/S and 50°-60° N/S are areas where temperature changes are the greatest. As the difference in temperature between the two locations increases, the strength of the wind increases. Therefore, the regions around 30° N/S and 50°-60° N/S are also regions where the wind in the upper atmosphere is the strongest.

Figure 8-4. Three Cell Circulations and Jet Stream Location

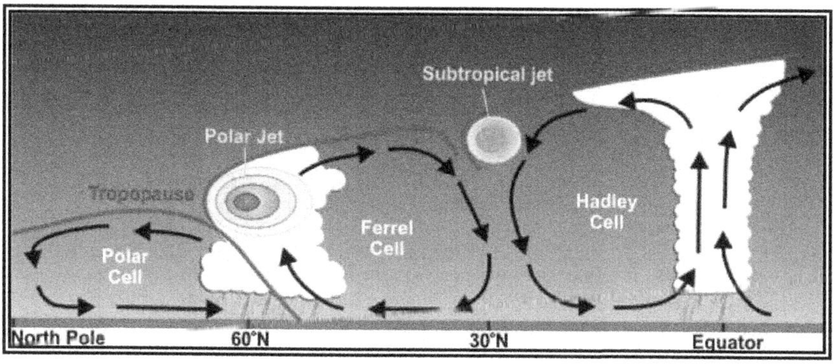

The 50°-60° N/S region is where the polar jet is located with the subtropical jet located around 30° N. Jet streams vary in height of 4 to 8 miles and can reach speeds of more than 275 miles per hour (239 knots /442 kilometers per hour).

Figure 8-5. Polar and Subtropical Jet Streams

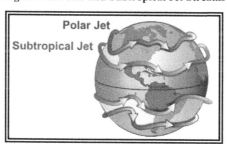

The actual appearance of jet streams results from the complex interaction between many variables, such as the location of high and low pressure systems, warm and cold air, and seasonal changes. They meander around the globe, dipping and rising in altitude/latitude, splitting at times and forming eddies, and even disappearing altogether to appear somewhere else.

Jet streams also follow the sun, in that as the sun's elevation increases each day in the spring, the jet streams shift north moving into Canada by summer. As autumn approaches and the sun's elevation decreases, the jet stream moves south into the United States, helping to bring cooler air to the country.

Figure 8-6. Jet Stream Wind Speeds

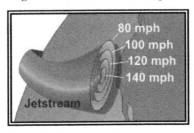

Also, the jet stream is often indicated by a line on maps, and shown by television meteorologists. The line generally points to the location of the strongest wind. In reality, jet streams are typically much wider. They are less a distinct location, and more a region where winds increase toward a core of highest speed.

One way of visualizing this is to consider a river. The river's current is generally the strongest in the center, with decreasing strength as one approaches the river's bank. It can be said that jet streams are rivers of air.

CHAPTER 9. LOCAL WINDS

9.1 **Description.** Local winds are small-scale wind field systems driven by diurnal heating or cooling of the ground. Air temperature differences develop over adjacent surfaces. Air in contact with the ground heats during the day and cools at night. Low-level pressure gradients develop with higher pressure over the cooler, denser air, and lower pressure over the warmer, less dense air (see Figure 9-1).

Figure 9-1. Local Wind Circulation

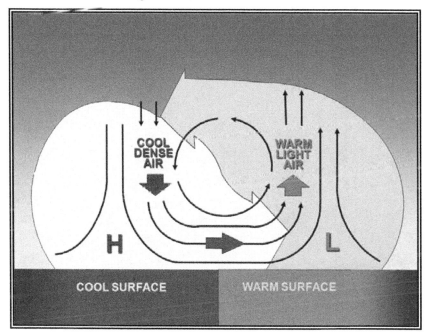

Low-level winds develop in the direction of the Pressure Gradient Force (PGF). Coriolis force is insignificant because the circulation's dimension (less than 100 miles) and life span (less than 12 hours) are too short for significant Coriolis deflection. Thus, the wind generally blows from a high-pressure cool surface to a low-pressure warm surface. Air rises over the warmer surface and sinks over the cooler surface. A local wind circulation is easiest to identify when synoptic-scale wind patterns are weak.

Local winds include: sea breeze, land breeze, lake breeze, lake effect, valley breeze, mountain-plains wind circulation, and mountain breeze.

9.2 **Hazards.** Local winds can produce aviation weather hazards. Turbulence and shifting surface winds are common. Clouds and precipitation (including thunderstorms) can develop in the rising air over the warmer surface given sufficient moisture and lift.

9.3 **Sea Breeze.** A sea breeze (see Figure 9-2) is a coastal local wind that blows from sea to land, and caused by temperature differences when the sea surface is colder than the adjacent land. Sea breezes usually blow on relatively calm, sunny, summer days.

Figure 9-2. Sea Breeze

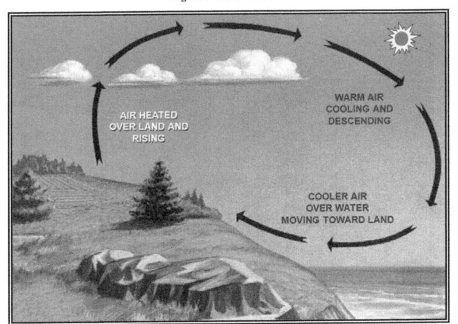

Air above the land becomes warmer (less dense) than air above the water. This is because land heats up faster than water. Low-level pressure gradients develop with lower pressure over the warmer land and higher pressure over the cooler water.

Low-level winds develop in the direction of the PGF. Thus, the wind blows from the water to the land. The air rises over land and sinks over water. Clouds (and precipitation) may develop in the rising air over land with cloud dissipation over the sinking air offshore.

9.3.1 Sea Breeze Front. A sea breeze front (see Figure 9-3) is the horizontal discontinuity in temperature and humidity that marks the leading edge of the intrusion of cooler, moister marine air associated with a sea breeze. It often produces a wind shift and enhanced cumulus clouds along its leading edge. Cumuliform clouds may be absent if the air mass being lifted over land is dry or stable.

Figure 9-3. Sea Breeze Front

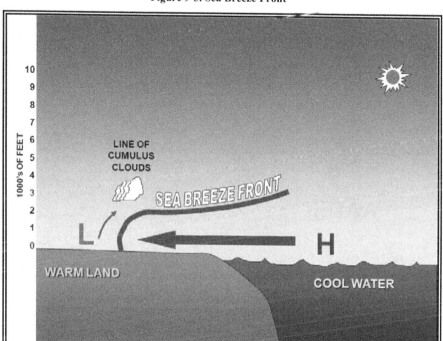

A sea breeze front's position and movement are influenced by coastline shape, low-level wind direction and speed, and temperature difference between land and sea surface. This temperature difference can be affected by the presence of cloud cover over land and the diurnal cycle. The depth of convection is usually too shallow for precipitation to develop. However, sea breeze fronts can be a lifting mechanism for shower and thunderstorm development.

9.3.2 Effects of Coastline Shape. Locally, the shape of the coastline plays an important role in the development of convection along sea breezes (see Figure 9-4). A narrow peninsula or island is generally an area of strong convective development during the late morning or early afternoon. This is because the sea breezes formed along opposing shores merge near the peninsula's or island's center.

Figure 9-4. Effects of Coastline Shape on a Sea Breeze

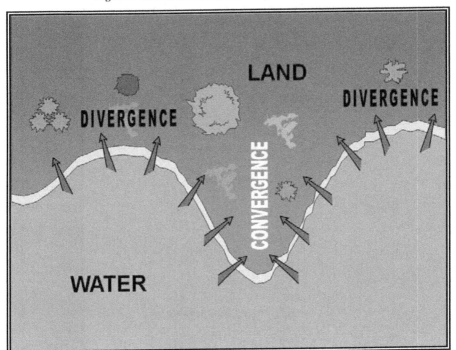

Convergence occurs where sea breezes merge from opposite directions. Stronger lift may be sufficient to initiate showers and thunderstorms if the air mass is sufficiently moist and unstable.

9.4 **Land Breeze.** A land breeze (see Figure 9-5) is a coastal breeze blowing from land to sea caused by the temperature difference when the sea surface is warmer than the adjacent land. Land breezes usually occur at night and during early morning.

Figure 9-5. Land Breeze

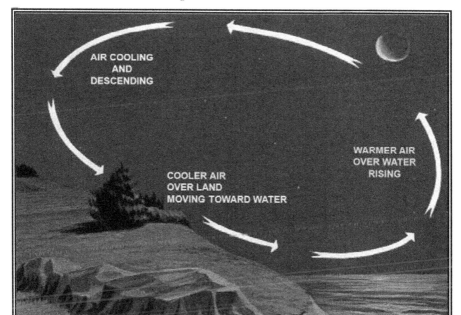

Air above the land becomes cooler (denser) than air above the water due to conduction. This is because land cools faster than water. Low-level pressure gradients develop with higher pressure over the cooler land and lower pressure over the warmer water.

Low-level winds develop in the direction of the PGF. Thus, the wind blows from the land to the water. The land breeze is usually weaker than the sea breeze. The air rises over water and sinks over land. Clouds and precipitation may develop in the rising air over the water.

9.5 **Lake Breeze.** A lake breeze (see Figure 9-6) is a local wind that blows from the surface of a large lake onto the shores during the afternoon and is caused by the temperature difference when the lake surface is colder than the adjacent land. The lake breeze is similar in origin to the sea breeze, and is common in the Great Lakes. Both occur during the warm season, primarily spring and summer. Both are easiest to detect in light synoptic wind conditions.

Figure 9-6. Lake Breeze

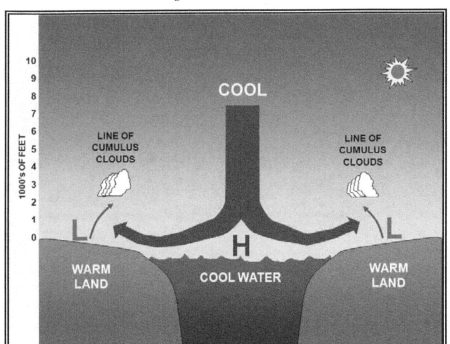

As with sea breezes, thunderstorms are favored in the upward motion branch of the lake breeze circulation. This is especially true where breezes from adjacent lakes collide.

The strength of the lake breeze circulation is affected by a lake's depth. A shallow lake (e.g., Lake Erie and Lake St. Clair) warms up rapidly and is less effective as the source of a lake breeze in summer than a deep lake (e.g., the other Great Lakes).

Figure 9-7. Sea Breeze/Lake Breeze Example

The sinking air behind the lake breeze inhibits clouds over Lake Ontario and Lake Erie and for miles inland (National Aeronautics and Space Administration (NASA)).

9.6 **Valley Breeze.** A valley breeze (see Figure 9-8) is a wind that ascends a mountain valley during the day. Air in contact with the sloping terrain becomes warmer (less dense) than air above the valley. This is because the air in contact with the sloping terrain heats up faster than air above the valley.

Figure 9-8. Valley Breeze

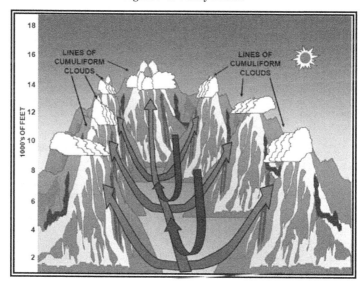

Pressure gradients develop (along a horizontal reference) with lower pressure over the warmer sloping terrain and higher pressure over the cooler valley winds develop in the direction of the PGF. Thus, the wind blows from the valley up the mountain slopes. Air rises over sloping terrain and sinks over the valley. Clouds and precipitation may develop over mountain slopes.

9.7 Mountain-Plains Wind System. A mountain-plains wind system (see Figure 9-9) is the diurnal cycle of local winds between a mountain or mountain range and the adjacent plains. During the daytime, this wind system is the equivalent of one-half of a valley breeze. Air in contact with the sloping terrain becomes warmer (less dense) than air above the plains. This is because the air in contact with the sloping terrain heats up faster than the air above the plains.

Figure 9-9. Mountain-Plains Wind System

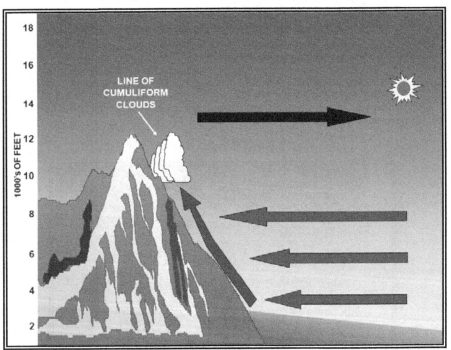

Pressure gradients develop (along a horizontal reference) with lower pressure over the warmer sloping terrain and higher pressure over the cooler plains. Winds develop in the direction of the PGF. Thus, the wind blows from the plains up the mountain slopes. There is a weak return flow aloft. Clouds and precipitation may develop in the rising air over the mountain.

9.8 Mountain Breeze. A mountain breeze (see Figure 9-10) is the nightly downslope winds commonly encountered in mountain valleys. Air in contact with the sloping terrain cools faster than air above the valley. Pressure over the sloping terrain is higher than over the valleys (along a horizontal reference). Cooler air over the sloping terrain is denser than warmer air over the valley.

Figure 9-10. Mountain Breeze

Surface wind flows from the mountain down the sloping terrain into the valley. Air rises over the valley and sinks over the sloping terrain.

CHAPTER 10. AIR MASSES, FRONTS, AND THE WAVE CYCLONE MODEL

10.1 **Air Masses.** An air mass is a large body of air with generally uniform temperature and humidity. The area from which an air mass originates is called a source region.

Air mass source regions range from extensive snow-covered polar areas to deserts to tropical oceans. The United States is not a favorable source region because of the relatively frequent passage of weather disturbances that disrupt any opportunity for an air mass to stagnate and take on the properties of the underlying region. The longer the air mass stays over its source region, the more likely it will acquire the properties of the surface below.

10.1.1 Air Mass Classification. Air masses are classified according to the temperature and moisture properties of their source regions (see Figure 10-1).

10.1.1.1 Temperature Properties:

- Arctic (A)—An extremely deep cold air mass which develops mostly in winter over arctic surfaces of ice and snow.
- Polar (P)—A relatively shallow cool to cold air mass which develops over high latitudes.
- Tropical (T)—A warm to hot air mass which develops over low latitudes.

10.1.1.2 Moisture Properties:

- Continental (c)—A dry air mass which develops over land.
- Maritime (m)—A moist air mass which develops over water.

10.1.1.3 Five Air Masses. When this classification scheme is applied, the following five air masses may be identified:

- Continental Arctic (cA)—Cold, dry.
- Continental Polar (cP)—Cold, dry.
- Continental Tropical (cT)—Hot, dry.
- Maritime Polar (mP)—Cool, moist.
- Maritime Tropical (mT)—Warm, moist.

Note: Maritime Arctic (mA) is not listed since it seldom, if ever, forms.

Figure 10-1. Air Mass Classification

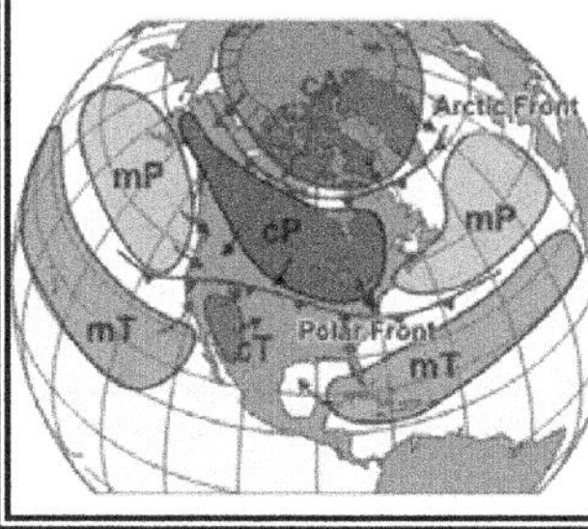

SOURCE REGION	Continental (c)	Maritime (m)
Arctic (A)	Continental Arctic (cA) (Cold, dry)	Not Applicable
Polar (P)	Continental Polar (cP) (Cold, dry)	Maritime Polar (mP) (Cool, moist)
Tropical (T)	Continental Tropical (cT) (Hot, dry)	Maritime Tropical (mT) (Warm, moist)

10.1.2 <u>Air Mass Modification</u>. As these air masses move around the Earth, they can begin to acquire different attributes. For example, in winter an arctic air mass (very cold and dry air) can move over the ocean, picking up some warmth and moisture from the warmer ocean and becoming a maritime polar (mP) air mass—one that is still fairly cold but contains moisture. If that same polar air mass moves south from Canada into the southern United States, it will pick up some of the warmth of the ground, but due to lack of moisture it remains very dry. This is called a continental polar (cP) air mass.

The Gulf Coast states and the eastern third of the country commonly experience the tropical air mass in the summer. Continental tropical (cT) air is dry air pumped north, off of the Mexican Plateau. If it becomes stagnant over the Midwest, a drought may result. Maritime tropical (mT) air is air from the tropics which has moved north over cooler water.

A warm, moist air mass moving over a cold surface (see Figure 10-2) produces stable air associated with stratiform clouds, fog, and drizzle.

Figure 10-2. Air Mass Modification—Warm, Moist Air Mass Moving Over a Cold Surface

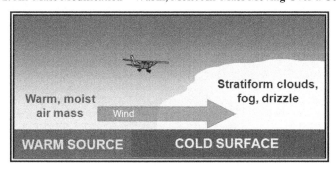

10.1.2.1 Lake Effect. Lake effect is the effect of any lake in modifying the weather near its shore and for some distance downwind. In the United States, the term is applied specifically to the region around the Great Lakes, and sometimes the Great Salt Lake in Utah. A lake effect can sometimes generate spectacular snowfall amounts to the lee of the Great Lakes. This phenomenon is termed lake effect snow.

In fall and winter, cumuliform clouds and showers often develop in bands over, and to the lee of, large, ice-free lakes (see Figure 10-3). As initially cold, dry, stable polar air over land flows over the relatively warm water, the air is heated and moistened, and stability decreases. Shallow cumuliform clouds develop with low tops. The strength of the convection increases with increasing temperature differences between warm water and cold air, increasing wind speeds, and decreasing relative humidity within the cold, dry air.

Figure 10-3. Lake Effect

10.2 Fronts. Air masses can control the weather for a relatively long time period ranging from days to months. Most weather occurs along the periphery of these air masses at boundaries called fronts. A front is a boundary or transition zone between two air masses. Fronts are classified by which type of air mass (cold or warm) is replacing the other (see Figure 10-4).

Figure 10-4. Fronts

FRONT	CHART SYMBOL	DEFINITION
Cold Front	 ▼▼	A front that moves in such a way that colder air replaces warmer air.
Warm Front	 ●●	A front that moves in such a way that warmer air replaces colder air.
Stationary Front	 ▼●	A front which is stationary or nearly so.
Occluded Front	▲●	A composite of two fronts as a cold front overtakes a warm front or stationary front.

Note: Frontal symbols point in the direction of frontal movement.

Fronts are usually detectable at the surface in a number of ways: significant temperature gradients, or differences, exist along fronts (especially on the cold air side); winds usually converge, or come together, at fronts; and pressure typically decreases as a front approaches and increases after it passes.

Fronts do not exist only at the surface of the Earth; they have a vertical structure in which the front slopes over the colder (denser) air mass. Cold fronts have a steep slope, and the warm air is forced upward abruptly (see Figure 10-5). This often leads to a narrow band of showers and thunderstorms along, or just ahead of, the front if the warm rising air is unstable. Warm fronts typically have a gentle slope, so the warm air rising along the frontal surface is gradual (see Figure 10-6). This favors the development of widespread layered or stratiform cloudiness and precipitation along, and ahead of, the front if the warm rising air is stable. Stationary frontal slope can vary, but clouds and precipitation would still form in the warm rising air along the front (see Figure 10-7).

Figure 10-5. Cold Front

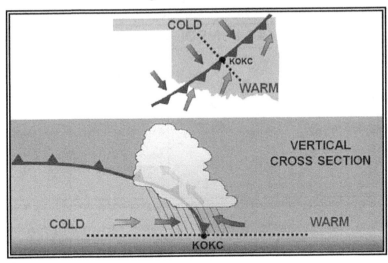

Figure 10-6. Warm Front

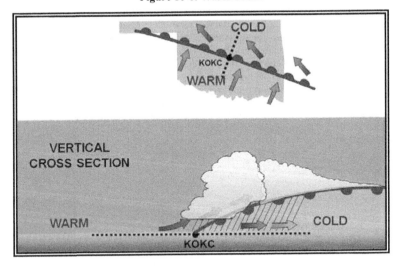

Figure 10-7. Stationary Front

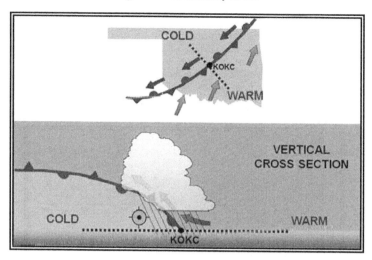

Cold fronts typically move faster than warm fronts, so in time they catch up to warm fronts. As the two fronts merge, an occluded front forms (see Figure 10-8). At the occluded front, the cold air undercuts the retreating cooler air mass associated with the warm front, further lifting the already rising warm air. Clouds and precipitation can occur in the areas of frontal lift along, ahead of, and behind the surface position of an occluded front.

Figure 10-8. Occluded Front

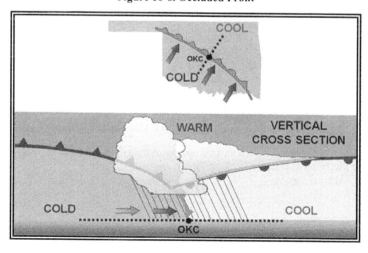

10.3 The Wave Cyclone Model. A wave cyclone[3] is a low pressure circulation that forms and moves along a front. The circulation about the cyclone center tends to produce a wavelike kink along the front. Wave cyclones are the primary weather producers in the mid-latitudes. They are large lows that generally travel from west to east along a front. They last from a few days to more than a week.

A wave cyclone typically follows a predictable evolution. Initially, there is a stationary front separating warm air from cold air (see Figure 10-9).

Figure 10-9. Wave Cyclone Model—Stage 1

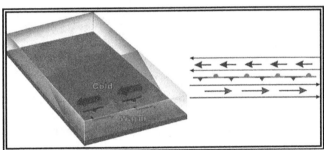

A low pressure wave forms on the front (see Figure 10-10). The front develops a kink where the wave develops. Precipitation develops with the heaviest intensity (dark green) located in the zone of lift along the front.

Figure 10-10. Wave Cyclone Model—Stage 2

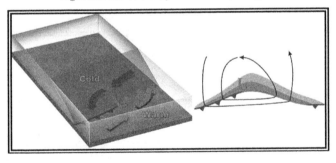

As the wave intensifies, both the cold and warm fronts become better organized (see Figure 10-11).

---

[3] A wave cyclone should not be confused with the alternative name for a tornado. They are quite different.

Figure 10-11. Wave Cyclone Model—Stage 3

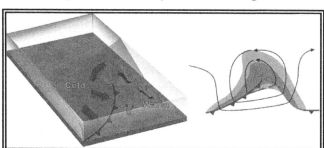

In the fourth stage, the wave becomes a mature low (see Figure 10-12). The occluded front forms as the cold front overtakes the warm front.

Figure 10-12. Wave Cyclone Model—Stage 4

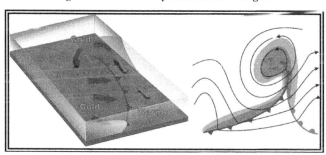

As the cold front continues advancing on the warm front, the occlusion increases and eventually cuts off the supply of warm moist air (see Figure 10-13). This causes the low to gradually dissipate.

Figure 10-13. Wave Cyclone Model—Stage 5

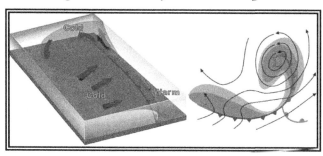

10.4 Dryline. A dryline is a low-level boundary hundreds of miles long separating moist and dry air masses. In the United States, it typically lies north-south across the southern and central High Plains during the spring and early summer, where it separates moist (mT) air from the Gulf of Mexico to the east and dry desert (cT) air from the southwestern states to the west (see Figure 10-14).

Figure 10-14. Dryline Example

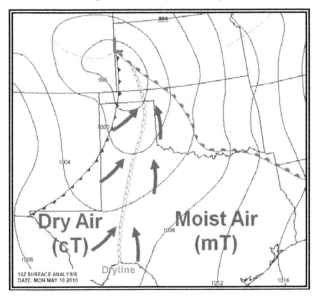

The dryline typically advances eastward during the afternoon and retreats westward at night. However, a strong wave cyclone can sweep the dryline eastward into the Mississippi Valley, or even further east, regardless of the time of day. Low-level clouds and early morning fog often prevail in the moist air, while generally clear skies mark the dry side. Severe and sometimes tornadic thunderstorms often develop along a dryline or in the moist air just to the east of it, especially when it begins moving eastward.

A typical dryline passage results in a sharp drop in humidity (hence the name), clearing skies, and a wind shift from south or southeasterly to west or southwesterly. Blowing dust and rising temperatures also may follow, especially if the dryline passes during the daytime. These changes occur in reverse order when the dryline retreats westward.

CHAPTER 11. VERTICAL MOTION AND CLOUD FORMATION

11.1 Introduction. A cloud is a visible aggregate of minute water droplets and/or ice particles in the atmosphere above the Earth's surface. Fog differs from cloud only in that the base of fog is at the Earth's surface while clouds are above the surface.

Clouds form in the atmosphere as a result of condensation of water vapor in rising currents of air, or by the evaporation of the lowest layer of fog. Rising currents of air are necessary for the formation of vertically deep clouds capable of producing precipitation heavier than light intensity.

11.2 Vertical Motion Effects on an Unsaturated Air Parcel. As a bubble or parcel of air ascends (rises), it moves into an area of lower pressure (pressure decreases with height). As this occurs, the parcel expands. This requires energy, or work, which takes heat away from the parcel, so the air cools as it rises (see Figure 11-1). This is called an adiabatic process. The term adiabatic means that no heat transfer occurs into, or out of, the parcel. Air has low thermal conductivity (see Table 2-3), so transfer of heat by conduction is negligibly small.

The rate at which the parcel cools as it is lifted is called the lapse rate. The lapse rate of a rising, unsaturated parcel (air with relative humidity less than 100 percent) is approximately 3 °C per 1,000 feet (9.8 °C per kilometer). This is called the dry adiabatic lapse rate. This means for each 1,000-foot increase in elevation, the parcel's temperature decreases by 3 °C. Concurrently, the dewpoint decreases approximately 0.5 °C per 1,000 feet (1.8 °C per kilometer). The parcel's temperature-dewpoint spread decreases, while its relative humidity increases.

This process is reversible if the parcel remains unsaturated and, thus, does not lose any water vapor. A descending (subsiding) air parcel compresses as it moves into an area of higher pressure. The atmosphere surrounding the parcel does work on the parcel, and energy is added to the compressed parcel, which warms it. Thus, the temperature of a descending air parcel increases approximately 3 °C per 1,000 feet (9.8 °C per kilometer). Concurrently, the dewpoint increases approximately 0.5 °C per 1,000 feet (1.8 °C per kilometer). The parcel's temperature-dewpoint spread increases, while its relative humidity decreases.

Figure 11-1. Unsaturated Ascending/Descending Air Parcel Example

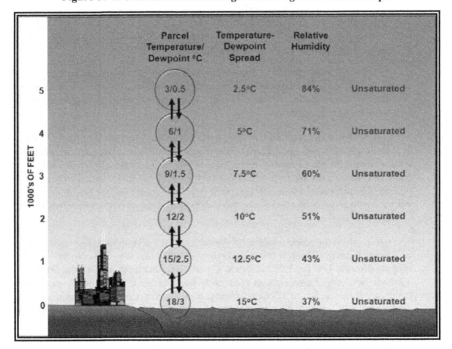

At the surface, the air parcel has a temperature of 18 °C and a dewpoint of 3 °C, which indicates that it is unsaturated. As the parcel ascends, its temperature decreases at the dry adiabatic lapse rate of 3 °C per 1,000 feet, while the dewpoint decreases at 0.5 °C per 1,000 feet. The temperature-dewpoint spread decreases while relative humidity increases. The process is reversible if the parcel remains unsaturated.

11.3 Vertical Motion Effects on a Saturated Air Parcel. The Lifting Condensation Level (LCL) is the level at which a parcel of moist air lifted dry adiabatically becomes saturated. At this altitude, the temperature-dewpoint spread is zero and relative humidity is 100 percent.

Further lifting of the saturated parcel results in condensation, cloud formation, and latent heat release. Because the heat added during condensation offsets some of the cooling due to expansion, the parcel now cools at the moist adiabatic lapse rate, which varies between approximately 1.2 °C per 1,000 feet (4 °C per kilometer) for very warm saturated parcels to 3 °C per 1,000 feet (9.8 °C per kilometer) for very cold saturated parcels. Concurrently, the parcel's dewpoint decreases at an identical rate. For simplicity, examples shown in this AC use a moist adiabatic lapse rate of 2 °C per 1,000 feet. Regardless of temperature, the relative humidity remains constant at about 100 percent.

As the saturated air parcel (see Figure 11-2) expands and cools, however, its water vapor content decreases. This occurs because some of the water vapor is condensed to water droplets or deposited into ice crystals to form a cloud. This process is triggered by the presence of microscopic cloud condensation (and ice) nuclei, such as dust, clay, soot, sulfate, and sea salt particles. The cloud grows vertically deeper as the parcel continues to rise.

Figure 11-2. Ascending Air Parcel that Becomes Saturated Example

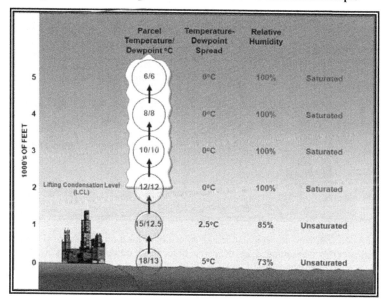

At the surface, the air parcel has a temperature of 18 °C and a dewpoint of 13 °C, which indicates that it is unsaturated. As the parcel ascends, its temperature decreases at the dry adiabatic lapse rate of 3 °C per 1,000 feet, while the dewpoint decreases at 0.5 °C per 1,000 feet. The temperature-dewpoint spread decreases while relative humidity increases until the parcel achieves saturation at its LCL of 2,000 feet. As the parcel continues to ascend, condensation produces cloud formation. Because the heat added during condensation offsets some of the cooling due to expansion, the parcel now cools at the moist adiabatic lapse rate of 2 °C per 1,000 feet. The parcel's dewpoint decreases at an identical rate as the lost water vapor condenses to form the cloud. The relative humidity of the ascending saturated (i.e., cloudy) parcel remains constant at about 100 percent.

A descending saturated air parcel (see Figure 11-3) quickly becomes unsaturated. Its temperature increases 3 °C per 1,000 feet, while its dewpoint increases at 0.5 °C per 1,000 feet (see Table 11-1). The temperature-dewpoint spread increases while relative humidity decreases.

Figure 11-3. Descending Air Parcel Example

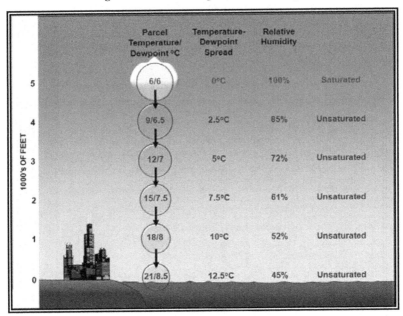

At 5,000 feet, both the temperature and dewpoint of the air parcel are 6 °C, which indicates that it is saturated. As the parcel descends, it quickly becomes unsaturated. Its temperature increases 3 °C per 1,000 feet, while its dewpoint increases at 0.5 °C per 1,000 feet. The temperature-dewpoint spread increases while relative humidity decreases until the parcel reaches the surface. Note that the parcel is now much warmer and drier at the surface then when it began the vertical motion process in Figure 11-2.

Table 11-1. Air Parcel Vertical Motion Characteristics

PARCEL	UNSATURATED			SATURATED		
	Temperature Change	Dewpoint Change	Relative Humidity	Temperature Change	Dewpoint Change	Relative Humidity
Ascending (rising)	-3 °C/1,000 ft	-0.5 °C/1,000 ft	Increases	-1.2 °C to -3 °C/1,000 ft	Identical to temperature change	100%
Descending (subsiding)	+3 °C/1,000 ft	+0.5 °C/1,000 ft	Decreases			

11.4 Common Sources of Vertical Motion. There are many sources of vertical motion in the atmosphere. Four of the most common types of vertical motion are orographic effects, frictional effects, frontal lift, and buoyancy.

11.4.1 <u>Orographic Effects</u>. Winds blowing across mountains and valleys cause the moving air to alternately ascend and descend. If relief is sufficiently great, the resulting expansional cooling and compressional warming of air affects the development and dissipation of clouds and precipitation.

For example, a mountain range that is oriented perpendicular to the prevailing wind flow forms a barrier that results in a cloudier and wetter climate on one side of the range than on the other side (see Figure 11-4). As air is forced to rise along the windward slope, it expands and cools, which increases its relative humidity. With sufficient cooling, clouds and precipitation develop at and above the LCL. Conversely, on the mountain's leeward slope, air descends and warms, which reduces its relative humidity, and tends to dissipate clouds and precipitation. In this way, mountain ranges induce two contrasting climatic zones: a moist climate on the windward slope and a dry climate on the leeward slope. Dry conditions often extend hundreds of miles to the lee of a prominent mountain range in a region known as rain shadow.

Figure 11-4. Orographic Effects Example

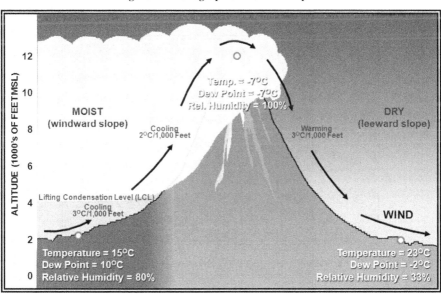

The air parcel begins with a temperature of 15 °C, dewpoint of 10 °C, and a relative humidity of 80 percent at 2,000 feet. As the parcel is lifted on the windward slope, the temperature cools at the dry adiabatic lapse rate of 3 °C per 1,000 feet and the dewpoint cools at a rate of 0.5 °C per 1,000 feet until it becomes saturated at the LCL at 4,000 feet. Then, the air parcel's temperature and dewpoint both cool at the moist adiabatic lapse rate of 2 °C per 1,000 feet until the parcel reaches the summit at 12,000 feet. At that altitude, the parcel's temperature is -7 °C, the dewpoint is 7 °C, and the relative humidity is 100 percent. As the air parcel descends the leeward slope, the temperature increases at a rate of 3 °C per 1,000 feet while the dewpoint increases 0.5 °C per 1,000 feet. The air parcel ends with a temperature of 23 °C, dewpoint of -2 °C, and a relative humidity of 33 percent at 2,000 feet, much warmer and drier than at the beginning.

Orographic effects are especially apparent from west to east across the Pacific Northwest, where the north-south Cascade Range intercepts the prevailing flow of humid air from the Pacific Ocean. Exceptionally cloudy, rainy weather prevails western slopes, whereas semiarid weather characterizes the eastern slopes and areas further east.

11.4.2 Frictional Effects. In the Northern Hemisphere, the surface wind spirals clockwise and outward from high pressure, and counterclockwise and inward into low pressure due to frictional force. The end result is that winds diverge away from surface high pressure, causing the air to sink, compress, and warm, which favors the dissipation of clouds and precipitation. Conversely, winds converge into surface low pressure, causing the air to rise, expand, and cool, which favors the formation of clouds and precipitation given sufficient moisture (see Figure 11-5).

Figure 11-5. Frictional Effects

11.4.3 Frontal Lift. Frontal lift (see Figure 11-6) occurs when the cold, denser air wedges under the warm, less dense air, plowing it upward, and/or the warmer air rides up and over the colder air in a process called overrunning. Cloud and precipitation will form given sufficient lift and moisture content of the warm air.

Figure 11-6. Frontal Lift

11.4.4 <u>Buoyancy</u>. Air near the ground can warm at different rates depending on the insular properties of the ground with which it is in contact. A newly plowed field will warm faster than an adjacent lake. These temperature differences result in different densities, allowing the warm air to become buoyant. The denser cool air will tend to push (i.e., lift) the less dense warm air aloft. On a grand scale, the tendency of air to rise due to heating, and how high it will rise, is referred to as stability and is covered in <u>Chapter 12</u>.

CHAPTER 12. ATMOSPHERIC STABILITY

12.1 Introduction. Convective clouds and precipitation pose a distinctly different flying environment than stratiform clouds and precipitation. These sharply contrasting conditions result from the atmosphere either resisting or accelerating the vertical motion of air parcels. Atmospheric stability is the property of the ambient air that either enhances or suppresses vertical motion of air parcels and determines which type of clouds and precipitation a pilot will encounter.

12.2 Using a Parcel as a Tool to Evaluate Stability. An air parcel can be used as a tool to evaluate atmospheric stability within a specified vertical column of air in the atmosphere. A parcel is selected from a specified altitude (usually the surface) and hypothetically lifted upward to a specified test altitude. As the parcel is lifted, its temperature decreases due to the expansion and latent heat effects discussed in Chapter 11.

The parcel and the surrounding environmental air temperatures are then compared. If the lifted parcel is colder than the surrounding air, it will be denser (heavier) and sink back to its original level. In this case, the parcel is stable because it resists upward displacement. If the lifted parcel is the same temperature as the surrounding air, it will be the same density and remain at the same level. In this case, the parcel is neutrally stable. If the lifted parcel is warmer and, therefore, less dense (lighter) than the surrounding air, it will continue to rise on its own until it reaches the same temperature as its environment. This final case is an example of an unstable parcel. Greater temperature differences result in greater rates of vertical motion.

12.3 Stability Types. The stability of a column of air in the atmosphere is classified by the distribution of parcel stabilities within the column. The Earth's surface is typically selected as the base while the top determines the column's depth. Five unique types of atmospheric stability can be identified.

12.3.1 Absolute Stability. Absolute stability (see Figure 12-1) is the state of a column of air in the atmosphere when its lapse rate of temperature is less than the moist adiabatic lapse rate. This includes both isothermal and inversion temperature profiles. An air parcel lifted upward would be colder (denser) than the surrounding environmental air and would tend to sink back to its level of origin.

Figure 12-1. Absolute Stability Example

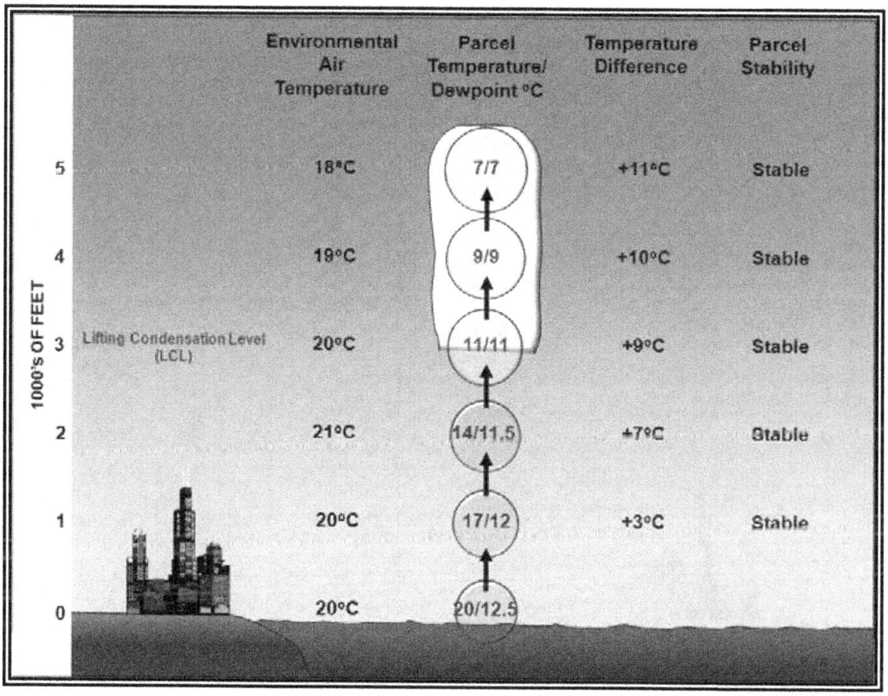

Altitude (1000's of feet)	Environmental Air Temperature	Parcel Temperature/ Dewpoint °C	Temperature Difference	Parcel Stability
5	18°C	7/7	+11°C	Stable
4	19°C	9/9	+10°C	Stable
3 (Lifting Condensation Level (LCL))	20°C	11/11	+9°C	Stable
2	21°C	14/11.5	+7°C	Stable
1	20°C	17/12	+3°C	Stable
0	20°C	20/12.5		

12.3.2 <u>Neutral Stability</u>. Neutral stability (see Figure 12-2) is the state of a column of air in the atmosphere in which an ascending (or descending) air parcel always has the same temperature (density) as the surrounding environmental air. If the column of air is unsaturated, then neutral stability exists when its lapse rate of temperature equals the dry adiabatic lapse rate. If the column of air is saturated, then neutral stability exists when its lapse rate of temperature equals the moist adiabatic lapse rate.

Figure 12-2. Neutral Stability Example

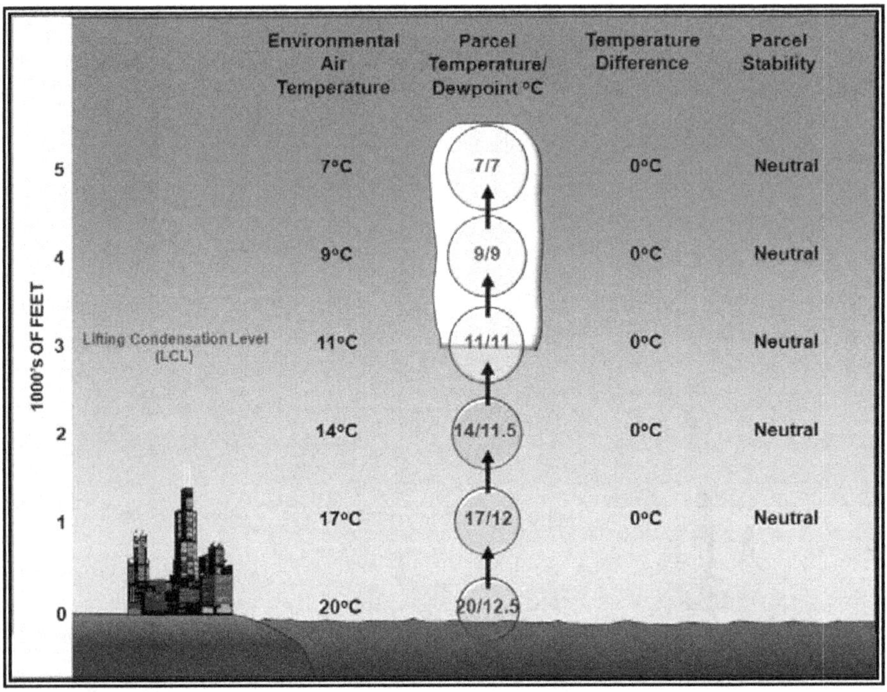

	Environmental Air Temperature	Parcel Temperature/ Dewpoint °C	Temperature Difference	Parcel Stability
5	7°C	7/7	0°C	Neutral
4	9°C	9/9	0°C	Neutral
3 (Lifting Condensation Level (LCL))	11°C	11/11	0°C	Neutral
2	14°C	14/11.5	0°C	Neutral
1	17°C	17/12	0°C	Neutral
0	20°C	20/12.5		

(1000's OF FEET)

12.3.3 <u>Absolute Instability</u>. Absolute instability (see Figure 12-3) is the state of a column of air in the atmosphere when it has a superadiabatic lapse rate of temperature (i.e., greater than the dry adiabatic lapse rate). An air parcel displaced vertically would be accelerated in the direction of the displacement. The kinetic energy of the parcel would consequently increase with increasing distance from its level of origin.

Figure 12-3. Absolute Instability Example

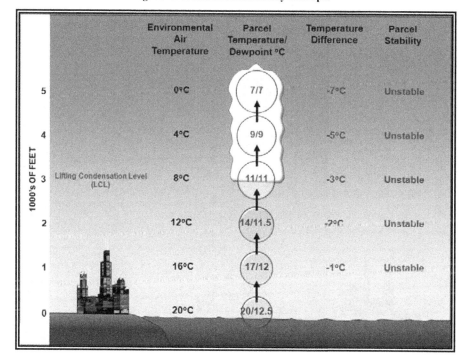

12.3.4 <u>Conditional Instability</u>. Conditional instability (see Figure 12-4) is the state of a column of unsaturated air in the atmosphere when its lapse rate of temperature is less than the dry adiabatic lapse rate, but greater than the moist adiabatic lapse rate. An air parcel lifted upward would be initially stable, but at some point above its Lifted Condensation Level (LCL) it would become unstable. The term conditional means the parcel must be lifted to a particular level (altitude) before it becomes unstable and rises because of its own buoyancy. The Level of Free Convection (LFC) is the level at which a parcel of air lifted dry adiabatically until saturated and moist adiabatically thereafter would first become warmer than the surrounding environmental air (i.e., unstable) in a conditionally unstable column of air in the atmosphere. The LFC is a defining feature of a conditionally unstable column of air.

Figure 12-4. Conditional Instability Example

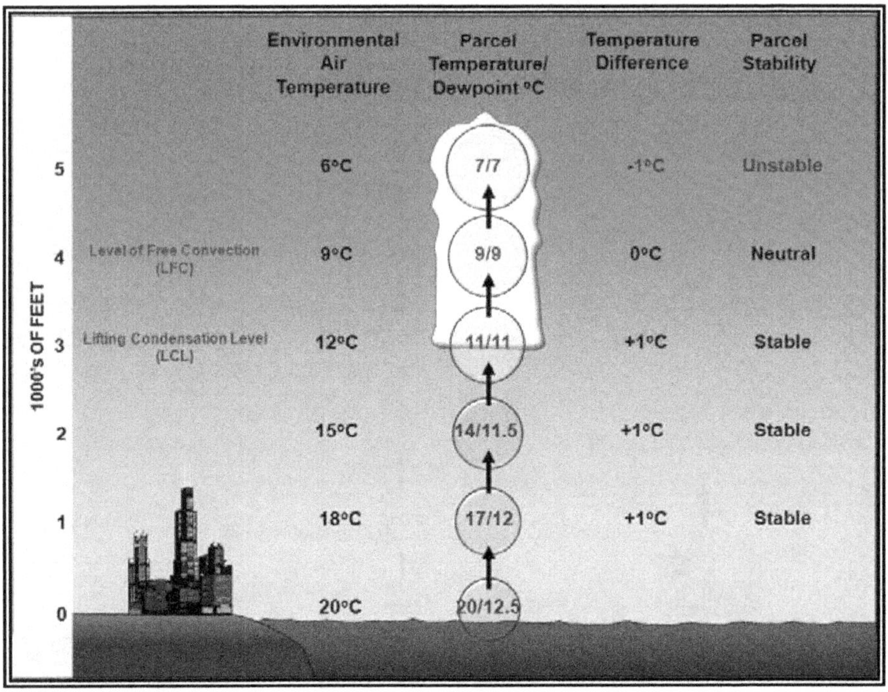

1000's OF FEET		Environmental Air Temperature	Parcel Temperature/ Dewpoint °C	Temperature Difference	Parcel Stability
5		6°C	7/7	-1°C	Unstable
4	Level of Free Convection (LFC)	9°C	9/9	0°C	Neutral
3	Lifting Condensation Level (LCL)	12°C	11/11	+1°C	Stable
2		15°C	14/11.5	+1°C	Stable
1		18°C	17/12	+1°C	Stable
0		20°C	20/12.5		

12.3.5 Summary of Stability Types. Figure 12-5 below summarizes the possible atmospheric stability types.

Figure 12-5. Stability Types

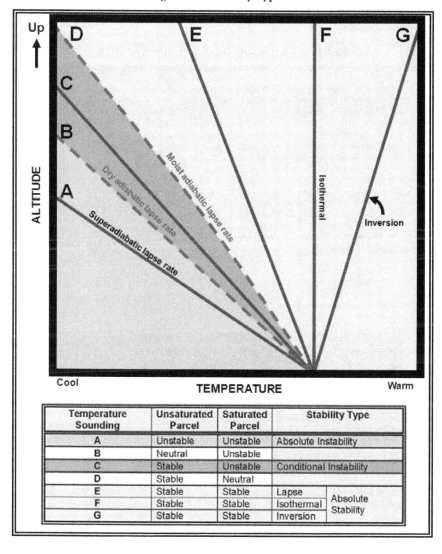

12.4 Processes that Change Atmospheric Stability. Changes in atmospheric stability are inversely related to temperature (density) changes with height (see Figure 12-6). If temperature lapse rates increase, then stability decreases. Conversely, if temperature lapse rates decrease, then stability increases. Most of these changes occur as a result of the movement of air, but diurnal (day/night) temperature variations can play a significant role.

Figure 12-6. Temperature Lapse Rate Effects on Stability

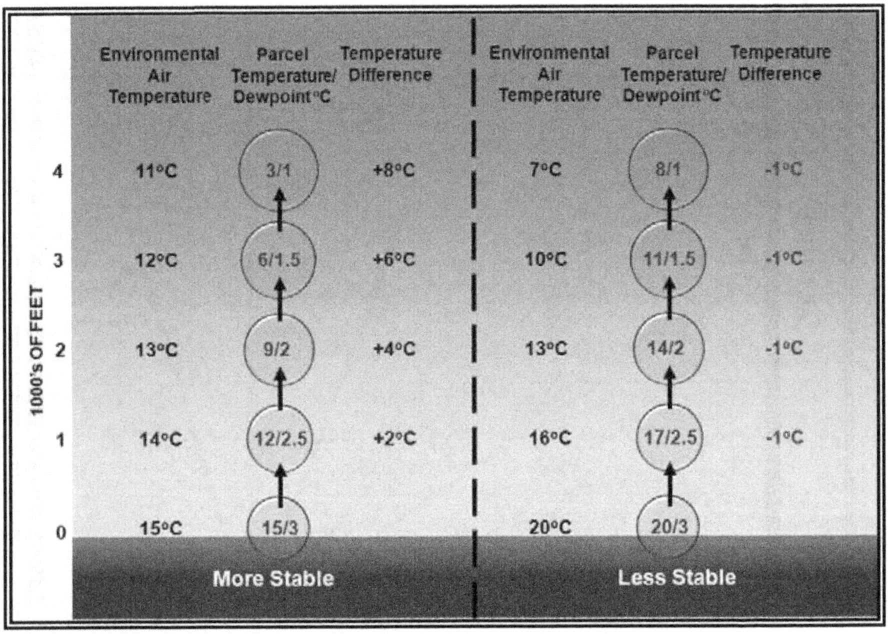

1000's OF FEET	Environmental Air Temperature	Parcel Temperature/ Dewpoint °C	Temperature Difference	Environmental Air Temperature	Parcel Temperature/ Dewpoint °C	Temperature Difference
4	11°C	3/1	+8°C	7°C	8/1	-1°C
3	12°C	6/1.5	+6°C	10°C	11/1.5	-1°C
2	13°C	9/2	+4°C	13°C	14/2	-1°C
1	14°C	12/2.5	+2°C	16°C	17/2.5	-1°C
0	15°C	15/3		20°C	20/3	
	More Stable			**Less Stable**		

The column of air on the right is less stable because its temperature lapse rate is higher.

12.4.1 <u>Wind Effects on Stability.</u> Wind can act to change the stability of a column of air in the atmosphere by changing the temperature lapse rate. Stability increases when wind blows colder air into the bottom of the air column (cold air advection) and/or warmer air at the top (warm air advection). Conversely, stability decreases when wind blows warmer air into the bottom of the air column and/or colder air at the top.

12.4.2 <u>Vertical Air Motion Effects on Stability.</u> A column of air in the atmosphere will become more stable when it descends (subsides) (see Figure 12-7). As it subsides, it becomes compressed by the weight of the atmosphere and shrinks vertically. The entire layer warms due to adiabatic compression. However, the upper part of the column sinks farther and, thus, warms more than the bottom part. This process acts to decrease the temperature lapse rate and increase stability.

Conversely, a column of air in the atmosphere will become less stable when it ascends (rises). As it rises, the rapid decrease in air density aloft causes the column to stretch out vertically. As long as the layer remains unsaturated, the entire layer cools at the dry adiabatic lapse rate (see Table 11-1). However, due to the stretching effect, air at the top of the column cools more than the air at the bottom of the column. This process acts to increase the temperature lapse rate and decrease stability.

Figure 12-7. Vertical Motion Effects on Stability

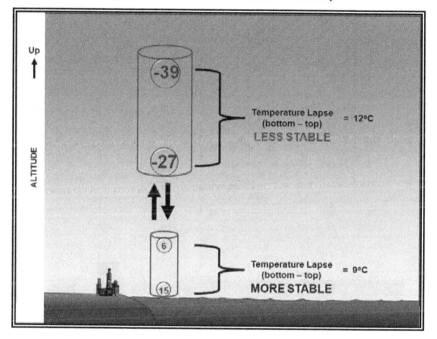

A rising column of air will become less stable when air at the bottom has a higher relative humidity than air at the top. As the air moves upward, the bottom becomes saturated first and cools at the lesser moist adiabatic lapse rate (see paragraph 11.2). The net effect is to increase the lapse rate within the column and decrease stability. This process is called convective instability, and is associated with the development of thunderstorms.

12.4.3 <u>Diurnal Temperature Variation Effects on Stability</u>. Diurnal (day/night) temperature variations (see Figure 12-8) can have a significant impact on atmospheric stability. Daytime heating of the surface increases temperature lapse rates and decreases stability. Conversely, nighttime cooling of the surface decreases temperature lapse rates and increases stability. Diurnal temperature variations are most pronounced in the lower troposphere because air is a poor conductor of heat (see Table 2-3).

The magnitude of diurnal temperature (and stability) variation is primarily influenced by surface type, latitude, sky cover (e.g., clouds and pollutants), water vapor content of the air, and wind speed. Temperature variation is maximized over land, at low latitudes, with a clear sky, dry air, and light wind. Conversely, temperature variation is minimized over large bodies of water, at high latitudes, with a cloudy sky, moist air, and strong wind.

Figure 12-8. Diurnal Temperature Variation Effects on Stability

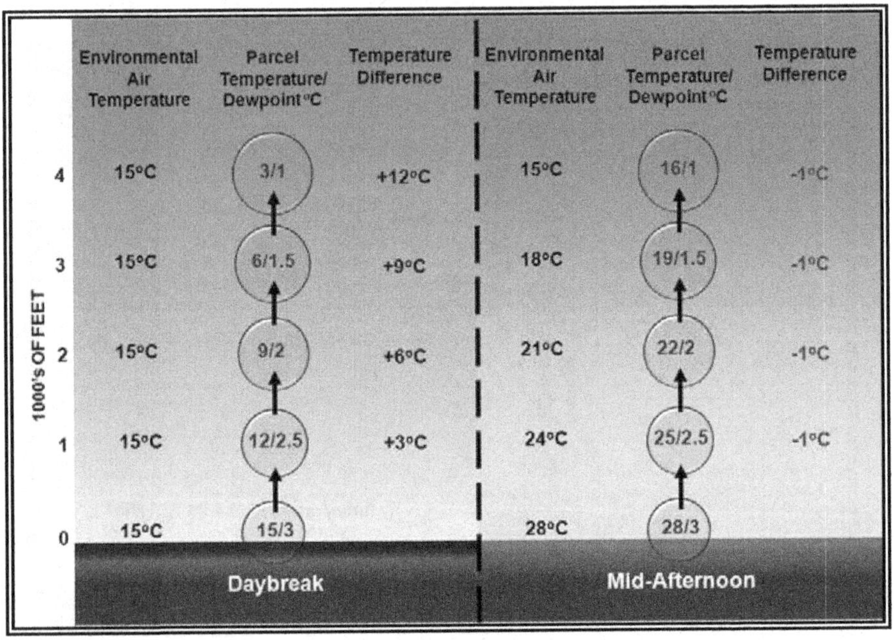

1000's OF FEET	Environmental Air Temperature	Parcel Temperature/ Dewpoint °C	Temperature Difference	Environmental Air Temperature	Parcel Temperature/ Dewpoint °C	Temperature Difference
4	15°C	3/1	+12°C	15°C	16/1	-1°C
3	15°C	6/1.5	+9°C	18°C	19/1.5	-1°C
2	15°C	9/2	+6°C	21°C	22/2	-1°C
1	15°C	12/2.5	+3°C	24°C	25/2.5	-1°C
0	15°C	15/3		28°C	28/3	
	Daybreak			**Mid-Afternoon**		

12.5 **Measurements of Stability.** Several stability indexes and other quantities exist that evaluate atmospheric stability and the potential for convective storms. The most common of these are Lifted Index (LI) and Convective Available Potential Energy (CAPE).

12.5.1 <u>Lifted Index.</u> The LI (see Figure 12-9) is the temperature difference between an air parcel (usually at the surface) lifted adiabatically (see Chapter 11) and the temperature of the environment at a given pressure (usually 500 millibars) in the atmosphere. A positive value indicates a stable column of air (at the respective pressure), a negative value indicates an unstable column of air, and a value of zero indicates a neutrally stable column of air. The larger the positive (negative) LI value, the more stable (unstable) the column of air.

LI is generally used in thunderstorm forecasting; however, CAPE is generally considered a superior measurement of instability. However, LI is easier to determine without using a computer.

Figure 12-9. Lifted Index Example

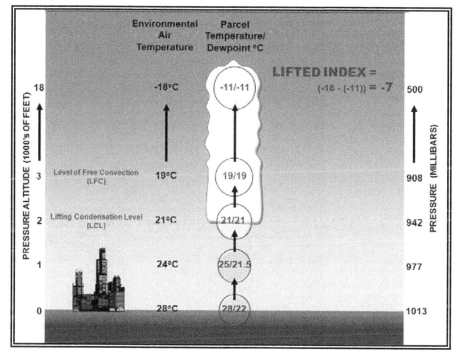

12.5.2 <u>Convective Available Potential Energy</u>. CAPE is the maximum amount of energy available to an ascending air parcel for convection. CAPE is represented on a sounding by the area enclosed between the environmental temperature profile and the path of a rising air parcel over the layer within which the latter is warmer than the former. Units are joules per kilogram of air (J/kg). Any value greater than 0 joules per kilogram indicates instability and the possibility of thunderstorms.

CAPE is directly related to the maximum potential vertical speed within an updraft; thus, higher values indicate the potential for stronger updrafts. Observed values in thunderstorm environments often exceed 1,000 joules per kilogram, and in extreme cases may exceed 5,000 joules per kilogram.

12.6 Summary. Atmospheric stability influences weather by affecting the vertical motion of air. Stable air suppresses vertical motion while unstable air enhances it. Chapter 13 will discuss how stability determines cloud and precipitation type.

CHAPTER 13. CLOUDS

13.1 Introduction. A cloud is a visible aggregate of minute water droplets and/or ice particles in the atmosphere above the Earth's surface. Fog differs from cloud only in that the base of fog is at the Earth's surface while clouds are above the surface. Clouds are like signposts in the sky that provide information on air motion, stability, and moisture. Clouds help pilots visualize weather conditions and potential weather hazards.

Clouds form in the atmosphere as a result of condensation of water vapor in rising currents of air, or by the evaporation of the lowest layer of fog. Rising currents of air are necessary for the formation of vertically deep clouds capable of producing precipitation heavier than light intensity, so we will focus on that process in this chapter.

13.2 Cloud Forms. There are four basic cloud forms (appearances) observed in the Earth's atmosphere (see Table 13-1).

Table 13-1. Cloud Forms

Cirriform	High-level clouds that form above 20,000 feet (0,000 meters) and are usually composed of ice crystals. High-level clouds are typically thin and white in appearance, but can create an array of colors when the sun is low on the horizon. Cirrus generally occur in fair weather and point in the direction of air movement at their elevation.
Nimbus	Nimbus comes from the Latin word meaning "rain." These clouds typically form between 7,000 and 15,000 feet (2,100 to 4,600 meters) and bring steady precipitation. As the clouds thicken and precipitation begins to fall, the bases of the clouds tend to lower toward the ground.
Cumuliform	Clouds that look like white, fluffy cotton balls or heaps and show the vertical motion or thermal uplift of air taking place in the atmosphere. The level at which condensation and cloud formation begins is indicated by a flat cloud base, and its height will depend upon the humidity of the rising air. The more humid the air, the lower the cloud base. The tops of these clouds can reach over 60,000 feet (18,000 meters).
Stratiform	Stratus is Latin for "layer" or "blanket." The clouds consist of a featureless low layer that can cover the entire sky like a blanket, bringing generally gray and dull weather. The cloud bases are usually only a few hundred feet above the ground. Over hills and mountains, they can reach ground level when they may be called fog. Also, as fog lifts off the ground due to daytime heating, the fog forms a layer of low stratus clouds.
From National Weather Service (NWS) Jetstream – Online School for Weather	

13.3 **Cloud Levels.** By convention, the part of the atmosphere in which clouds are usually present has been divided into three levels: high, middle, and low (see Table 13-2). Each level is defined by the range of heights at which the cloud of a certain type occurs most frequently. The levels overlap and their limits vary with latitude. The approximate heights of the limits are as follows:

Table 13-2. Approximate Height of Cloud Bases above the Surface

LEVEL	POLAR REGIONS	TEMPERATE REGIONS	TROPICAL REGIONS
High Clouds	10,000-25,000 ft (3-8 km)	16,500-40,000 ft (5-13 km)	20,000-60,000 ft (6-18 km)
Middle Clouds	6,500-13,000 ft (2-4 km)	6,500-23,000 ft (2-7 km)	6,500-25,000 ft (2-8 km)
Low Clouds	Surface-6,500 ft (0-2 km)	Surface-6,500 ft (0-2 km)	Surface-6,500 ft (0-2 km)

13.4 **Cloud Types.** In each level, the clouds may be divided by type (genera). The definitions of the cloud types (given below) do not cover all possible aspects, but are limited to a description of the main types and of the essential characteristics necessary to distinguish a given type from another type having a somewhat similar appearance.

Clouds are identified based upon one's observation point at a particular elevation. From sea level, one might observe stratus clouds enveloping the top of a mountain. However, on the mountaintop, one would observe and report that same cloud as fog.

The exception to this is cumulus or cumulonimbus clouds over a mountain. Even though these low-level clouds typically have bases under 6,500 feet (2,000 meters), if one were to observe them over a mountaintop, their base might be 12,000 feet (3,600 meters) or higher relative to a particular location closer to sea level. However, due to their location over the mountain, one would still call them cumulus or cumulonimbus clouds, as appropriate.

13.4.1 High Clouds. Cirrus (Ci), Cirrocumulus (Cc), and Cirrostratus (Cs) are high-level clouds. They are typically thin and white in appearance, but can appear in a magnificent array of colors when the sun is low on the horizon. They are composed almost entirely of ice crystals.

13.4.1.1 **Cirrus (Ci).** Cirrus (Ci) (see Figure 13-1) is a cloud type composed of detached cirriform elements in the form of white, delicate filaments of white (or mostly white) patches, or of narrow bands. These clouds have a fibrous (hair-like) appearance and/or a silky sheen. Many of the ice crystal particles of cirrus are sufficiently large to acquire an appreciable speed of fall;

therefore, the cloud elements often trail downward in well-defined wisps called mares' tails. Cirrus clouds in themselves have little effect on aircraft and contain no significant icing or turbulence.

Figure 13-1. Cirrus (Ci)

13.4.1.2 **Cirrocumulus (Cc).** Cirrocumulus (Cc) is a cirriform cloud type appearing as a thin, white patch, sheet, or layer of cloud without shading, and is composed of very small elements in the form of grains, ripples, etc. The elements may be merged or separate, and more or less regularly arranged; they subtend an angle of less than 1° when observed at an angle of more than 30° above the horizon.

Cirrocumulus (see Figure 13-2) may be composed of highly supercooled[4] water droplets, as well as small ice crystals, or a mixture of both; usually, the droplets are rapidly replaced by ice crystals. Pilots can expect some turbulence and icing.

---

[4] Supercooled water droplets are below freezing. Even though their temperature is below the freezing point, they have not turned into ice. See paragraph 18.2 and paragraph 18.3.2.1.

Figure 13-2. Cirrocumulus (Cc)

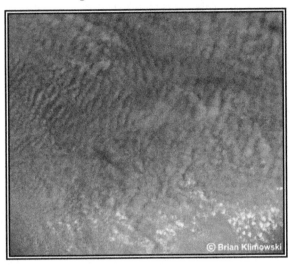

Cirrocumulus is not very common. It is composed of very small elements, which never show shading. The cloud is frequently associated with cirrus or cirrostratus.

13.4.1.3 **Cirrostratus (Cs).** Cirrostratus (Cs) (see Figure 13-3) is a cloud type appearing as a whitish veil, usually fibrous (hair-like) but sometimes smooth, that may totally cover the sky, and that often produces halo phenomena, either partial or complete. Cirrostratus occasionally may be so thin and transparent as to render it nearly indiscernible, especially through haze or at night. At such times, the existence of a halo around the sun or moon may be the only revealing feature.

The angle of incidence of illumination upon a cirrostratus layer is an important consideration in evaluating the identifying characteristics. When the sun is high (generally above 50° elevation), cirrostratus never prevents the casting of shadows by terrestrial objects, and a halo might be completely circular. At progressively lower angles of the sun, halos become fragmentary, and light intensity noticeably decreases. When near the horizon, cirrostratus may be impossible to distinguish from cirrus.

Cirrostratus clouds are composed primarily of ice crystals and contain little, if any, icing and no turbulence.

Figure 13-3. Cirrostratus (Cs)

13.4.2 <u>Middle Clouds</u>. Altocumulus (Ac), Altostratus (As), and Nimbostratus (Ns) are mid-level clouds. They are composed primarily of water droplets; however, they can also be composed of supercooled liquid water droplets and/or ice crystals when temperatures are below freezing. Altostratus is usually found in the middle level, but it often extends higher. Nimbostratus is almost invariably found in the middle level, but it usually extends into the other levels.

    13.4.2.1 **Altocumulus (Ac).** Altocumulus (Ac) (see Figure 13-4) is a cloud type, white and/or gray in color, that occurs as a layer or patch with a waved aspect, the elements of which appear as laminae, rounded masses, rolls, etc. These elements usually are sharply outlined, but they may become partly fibrous or diffuse; they may or may not be merged.

    Small liquid water droplets invariably compose the major part of the composition of altocumulus. This results in a sharp outline and small internal visibility. At very low temperatures, however, ice crystals may form. Pilots flying through altocumulus can expect some turbulence and small amounts of icing.

Figure 13-4. Altocumulus (Ac)

This altocumulus is a single level, the greater part of which is sufficiently transparent to reveal the position of the sun and moon. The clouds do not progressively invade the sky, and the individual elements change very little. These thin altocumulus clouds usually produce a corona.

13.4.2.1.1 Altocumulus Lenticularis. Altocumulus Lenticularis, commonly known as Altocumulus Standing Lenticular (ACSL) (see Figure 13-5), are an orographic type of cloud. They often appear to be dissolving in some places and forming in others. They also often form in patches in the shape of almonds or wave clouds. These formations are caused by wave motions in the atmosphere and are frequently seen in mountainous or hilly areas. They may be triggered off by hills only a few thousand feet high and may extend downwind for more than 60 miles (100 kilometers). The cloud elements form at the windward edge of the cloud and are carried to the downwind edge where they evaporate. The cloud as a whole is usually stationary or slow moving. These clouds often have very smooth outlines and show definite shading.

The ACSL clouds indicate the position of the wave crests, but they do not necessarily give an indication on the intensity of turbulence or strength of updrafts and downdrafts. This is because the clouds depend on both lifting and moisture. A well-defined wave may be visible (i.e., ACSL cloud) in weak updrafts where there is an adequate supply of moisture, but may not be visible when the environment is very dry, even if the wave is intense.

Figure 13-5. Altocumulus Standing Lenticular (ACSL)

13.4.2.2 **Altostratus (As).** Altostratus (As) (see Figure 13-6) is a cloud type in the form of a gray or bluish (never white) sheet or layer of striated, fibrous, or uniform appearance. Altostratus very often totally covers the sky and may, in fact, cover an area of several thousand square miles. The layer has parts thin enough to reveal the position of the sun, and if gaps and rifts appear, they are irregularly shaped and spaced.

Within the rather large vertical extent of altostratus (from several hundred to thousands of feet), a very heterogeneous particulate composition may exist. In this most complete case, there may be distinguished: 1) an upper part, mostly or entirely ice crystals; 2) a middle part, a mixture of ice crystals and/or snowflakes and supercooled water droplets; and 3) a lower part, mostly or entirely supercooled or ordinary water droplets. A number of partial combinations of these composition types may occur, but never an entire cloud like 3) above. The particles are widely dispersed enough so as not to obscure the sun except by its thickest parts, but rather to impose a ground-glass effect upon the sun's image, and to prevent sharply outlined shadows from being cast by terrestrial objects. Halo phenomena do not occur. Pilots can expect little or no turbulence, but light to moderate icing in the supercooled water regions.

Figure 13-6. Thin Altostratus (As)

Thin altostratus usually evolves from the gradual thickening of a veil of cirrostratus. This means that unlike most clouds which increase in height as they grow, altostratus (and nimbostratus) grow as the base of the cloud lowers. Altostratus is grayish or bluish color, never white, and the greater part is always translucent enough to reveal the sun (or moon) as through ground glass. Objects on the ground do not cast shadows and halo phenomena are never seen.

13.4.2.3 **Nimbostratus (Ns).** Nimbostratus (Ns) is a gray cloud layer, often dark, rendered diffuse by more or less continuously falling rain, snow, ice pellets, etc., which in most cases reaches the ground. It is not accompanied by lightning, thunder, or hail.

Nimbostratus is composed of suspended water droplets, sometimes supercooled, and of falling raindrops and/or snow crystals or snowflakes. It occupies a layer of large horizontal and vertical extent. The great density and thickness (usually many thousands of feet) of this cloud prevent observation of the sun. This, plus the absence of small droplets in its lower portion, gives nimbostratus the appearance of dim and uniform lighting from within. It also follows that nimbostratus has no well-defined base, but rather a deep zone of visibility attenuation. Frequently a false base may appear at the level where snow melts into rain. It is officially classified as a middle cloud although it may merge into very low stratus or stratocumulus. Other cloud classification systems may identify it as a low-level cloud. Nimbostratus produces very little turbulence, but can pose a serious icing problem if temperatures are near or below freezing.

Figure 13-7. Thick Altostratus (As) or Nimbostratus (Ns)

Thick altostratus is denser and of a darker gray or bluish gray than thin altostratus with the greater part sufficiently dense to completely mask the sun or moon. With further thickening of the altostratus and a lowering of its base, the cloud may begin to produce precipitation, at which point it is called nimbostratus. Some cloud charts will depict nimbostratus as a low-level cloud. This is because oftentimes, during continuously falling precipitation, the base of nimbostratus clouds decrease into the low level. But officially and historically, nimbostratus is classified as a mid-level cloud.

13.4.3 <u>Low Clouds</u>. Cumulus (Cu), Towering cumulus (TCu), Stratocumulus (Sc), Stratus (St), and Cumulonimbus (Cb) are low clouds composed of water droplets. However, they can also be composed of supercooled liquid water droplets and/or ice crystals when temperatures are below freezing. Cumulus and Cumulonimbus usually have bases in the low level, but their vertical extent is often so great that their tops may reach into the middle and high levels.

    13.4.3.1 Cumulus (Cu) and Towering Cumulus (TCu). Cumulus is a cloud type in the form of individual, detached elements that are generally dense and possess sharp, nonfibrous outlines. These elements develop vertically, appearing as rising mounds, domes, or towers, the upper parts of which often resemble a cauliflower. The sunlit parts of these clouds are mostly brilliant white; their bases are relatively dark and nearly horizontal. Near the horizon, the vertical development of cumulus often causes the individual clouds to appear merged. If precipitation occurs, it is usually of a showery nature. Various effects of wind, illumination, etc., may modify many of the above characteristics.

Cumulus is composed of a great density of small water droplets, frequently supercooled. Within the cloud, larger water drops are formed that may, as the cloud develops, fall from the base as rain or virga.[5] Ice crystal formation will occur within the cloud at sufficiently low temperatures, particularly in upper portions as the cloud grows vertically.

For cumulus with little vertical development, pilots can expect some turbulence and no significant icing. However, for towering cumulus (i.e., cumulus of moderate/strong development) pilots can expect very strong turbulence and some clear icing above the freezing level (where temperatures are negative). Towering cumulus is also referred to as the first stage of a thunderstorm.

Figure 13-8. Cumulus (Cu) with Little Vertical Development

Cumulus formation is often preceded by hazy spots out of which the clouds evolve. When completely formed, the clouds have clear-cut horizontal bases and flattened or slightly rounded tops. At this stage of development, they are known as fair weather cumulus. Over land, on clear mornings, cumulus may form as the sun rapidly heats the ground. Near coasts, cumulus may form over the land by day in a sea breeze and over the sea during the night in a land breeze.

---

[5] Virga are wisps or streaks of water or ice particles falling out of a cloud, but vaporizing before reaching the Earth's surface as precipitation.

Figure 13-9. Towering Cumulus (TCu)

13.4.3.2 Stratocumulus (Sc). Stratocumulus (Sc) (see Figure 13-10) is a cloud type, predominantly stratiform, in the form of a gray and/or whitish layer or patch, which nearly always has dark parts and is nonfibrous (except for virga). Its elements are tessellated, rounded, roll-shaped, etc.; they may or may not be merged, and usually are arranged in orderly groups, lines, or undulations, giving the appearance of a simple (or occasionally a cross pattern) wave system. These elements are generally flat-topped, smooth, and large; observed at an angle of more than 30° above the horizon, the individual stratocumulus element subtends an angle of greater than 5°. When a layer is continuous, the elemental structure is revealed in true relief on its undersurface.

Stratocumulus is composed of small water droplets, sometimes accompanied by larger droplets, soft hail, and (rarely) by snowflakes. Under ordinary conditions, ice crystals are too sparse even to give the cloud a fibrous aspect; however, in extremely cold weather, ice crystals may be numerous enough to produce abundant virga, and sometimes even halo phenomena. The highest liquid water contents are in the tops of these clouds where the icing threat is the greatest, if cold enough. Virga may form under the cloud, particularly at very low temperatures. Precipitation rarely occurs with stratocumulus.

Pilots can expect some turbulence and possible icing at subfreezing temperatures. Ceiling and visibility are usually better than with low stratus.

Figure 13-10. Stratocumulus (Sc)

This stratocumulus occurs in patches or layers, composed of rounded masses or rolls, at one or more levels. The clouds are gray or whitish and always have dark parts. Sometimes the elements lie in parallel bands. Due to perspective these may appear to converge towards the horizon. It may also occur in the shape of lenses or almonds, although this is fairly rare.

13.4.3.3 **Stratus (St).** Stratus (St) (see Figure 13-11 and Figure 13-12) is a cloud type in the form of a gray layer with a fairly uniform base. Stratus does not usually produce precipitation, but when it does occur, it is in the form of minute particles, such as drizzle, ice crystals, or snow grains. Stratus often occurs in the form of ragged patches or cloud fragments, in which case rapid transformation is a common characteristic. When the sun is seen through the cloud, its outline is clearly discernible. In the immediate area of the solar disk, stratus may appear very white. Away from the sun, and at times when the cloud is sufficiently thick to obscure it, stratus gives off a weak, uniform luminance.

The particulate composition of stratus is quite uniform, usually of fairly widely dispersed water droplets and, at lower temperatures, of ice crystals (although this is much less common). Halo phenomena may occur with this latter composition.

Stratus produces little or no turbulence, but temperatures near or below freezing can create hazardous icing conditions. When stratus is associated with fog or precipitation, the combination can become troublesome for visual flying.

Figure 13-11. Stratus (St)

Stratus most commonly occurs as a gray, fairly uniform, and featureless single layer of low cloud. Occasionally it can be dark or threatening, although at most it can only produce weak precipitation. This feature makes it fairly easy to distinguish it from nimbostratus (Ns), which nearly always produces rain, snow, or ice pellets. Fog will often lift into a layer of stratus by an increase in wind or a rise in temperature. Stratus is sometimes comparatively thin, and the disk of the sun or moon may be seen with a clear outline.

Figure 13-12. Stratus Fractus (StFra) and/or Cumulus Fractus (CuFra) of Bad Weather

These ragged shreds of low cloud always appear in association with other clouds for a short time before, during, and a short time after precipitation. They often form beneath lowering altostratus (As) or nimbostratus (Ns). They also occur beneath cumulonimbus (Cb) and precipitating cumulus (Cu) and are collectively known as scud clouds.

    13.4.3.4   **Cumulonimbus (Cb).** A cumulonimbus (Cb) (see Figure 13-13 and Figure 13-14) is a cloud type, exceptionally dense and vertically developed, occurring either as isolated clouds or as a line or wall of clouds with separated upper portions. These clouds appear as mountains or huge towers, at least a part of the upper portions of which are usually smooth, fibrous, or striated, and almost flattened as it approaches the tropopause. This part often spreads out in the form of an anvil or vast plume. Under the base of cumulonimbus, which is often very dark, there frequently exist virga, precipitation, and low, ragged clouds, either merged with it or not. Its precipitation is often heavy and always of a showery nature. The usual occurrence of lightning and thunder within or from this cloud leads to its popular appellations: thundercloud, thunderhead (the latter usually refers only to the upper portion of the cloud), and thunderstorm.

                Cumulonimbus is composed of water droplets and ice crystals, the latter almost entirely in its upper portions. It also contains large water drops, snowflakes, snow pellets, and sometimes hail. The liquid water forms may be substantially supercooled. Cumulonimbus contains nearly the entire spectrum of flying hazards, including extreme turbulence.

Figure 13-13. Cumulonimbus (Cb) Without Anvil

No part of the cloud top has acquired a fibrous appearance or any anvil development. The protuberances tend to form a whitish mass without striations. Showers or thunderstorms may occur. The presence of lightning/thunder differentiate between this cloud and towering cumulus. Cumulus, stratocumulus, or stratus may also be present.

Figure 13-14. Cumulonimbus (Cb) with Anvil

The characteristic shape of these clouds can only be seen as a whole when viewed from a distance. The tops of these massive clouds show a fibrous or striated structure that frequently resembles an anvil, plume, or huge mass of hair. They may occur as an isolated cloud or an extensive wall and squalls, hail, and/or thunder often accompany them. Underneath the base, which is often very dark, stratus fractus frequently form and, in storms, these may be only a few hundred feet above the Earth's surface, and they can merge to form a continuous layer. Mammatus may form, especially on the underside of the projecting anvil, and may appear particularly prominent when the sun is low in the sky. A whole variety of other clouds, such as dense cirrus, altocumulus, altostratus, stratocumulus, cumulus, and stratus may also be present.

CHAPTER 14. PRECIPITATION

14.1 **Introduction.** Precipitation is any of the forms of water particles, whether liquid or solid, that fall from the atmosphere and reach the ground. The precipitation types are: drizzle, rain, snow, snow grains, ice crystals, ice pellets, hail, and small hail and/or snow pellets.

14.2 **Necessary Ingredients for Formation.** Precipitation formation requires three ingredients: water vapor, sufficient lift to condense the water vapor into clouds, and a growth process that allows cloud droplets to grow large and heavy enough to fall as precipitation. Significant precipitation usually requires clouds to be at least 4,000 feet thick. The heavier the precipitation, the thicker the clouds are likely to be. When arriving or departing from an airport reporting precipitation of light or greater intensity, expect clouds to be more than 4,000 feet thick.

14.3 **Growth Process.** All clouds contain water, but only some produce precipitation. This is because cloud droplets and/or ice crystals are too small and light to fall to the ground as precipitation. Because of their microscopic size, the rate at which cloud droplets fall is incredibly slow. An average cloud droplet falling from a cloud base at 3,300 feet (1,000 meters) would require about 48 hours to reach the ground. It would never complete this journey because it would evaporate within minutes after falling below the cloud base. Two growth processes exist which allow cloud droplets (or ice crystals) to grow large enough to reach the ground as precipitation before they evaporate (or sublimate). One process is called the collision-coalescence, or warm rain process (see Figure 14-1). In this process, collisions occur between cloud droplets of varying size and different fall speeds, sticking together or coalescing to form larger drops. Finally, the drops become too large to be suspended in the air, and they fall to the ground as rain. This is thought to be the primary growth process in warm, tropical air masses where the freezing level is very high.

Figure 14-1. The Collision-Coalescence or Warm Rain Process

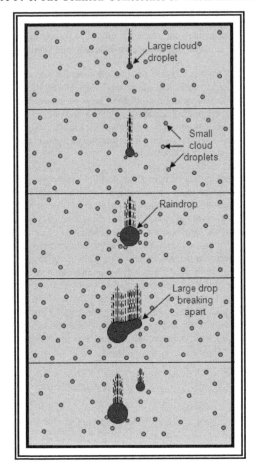

Most cloud droplets are too small and light to fall to the ground as precipitation. However, the larger cloud droplets fall more rapidly and are able to sweep up the smaller ones in their path and grow.

The other process is the ice crystal process. This occurs in colder clouds when both ice crystals and water droplets are present. In this situation, it is easier for water vapor to deposit directly onto the ice crystals so the ice crystals grow at the expense of the water droplets. The crystals eventually become heavy enough to fall. If it is cold near the surface, it may snow; otherwise, the snowflakes may melt to rain. This is thought to be the primary growth process in mid- and high-latitudes.

14.4 Precipitation Types. The vertical distribution of temperature will often determine the type of precipitation that occurs at the surface. Snow occurs when the temperature remains below freezing throughout the entire depth of the atmosphere (see Figure 14-2).

Figure 14-2. Snow Temperature Environment

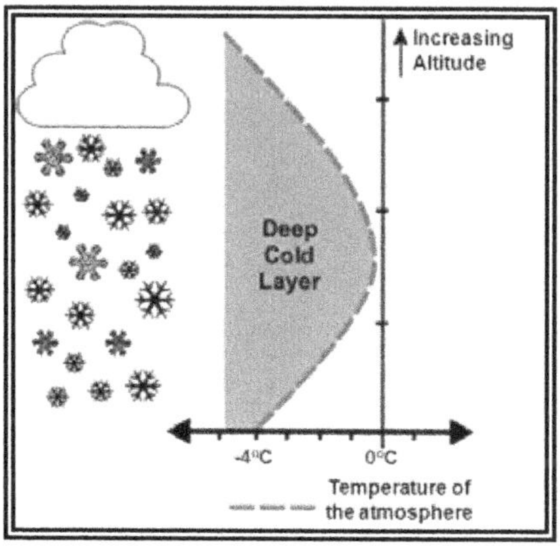

Ice pellets (sleet) occur when there is a shallow layer aloft with above freezing temperatures and with a deep layer of below freezing air based at the surface. As snow falls into the shallow warm layer, the snowflakes partially melt. As the precipitation reenters air that is below freezing, it refreezes into ice pellets (see Figure 14-3).

Figure 14-3. Ice Pellets Temperature Environment

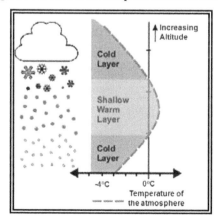

Freezing rain occurs when there is a deep layer aloft with above freezing temperatures and with a shallow layer of below freezing air at the surface. It can begin as either rain and/or snow, but becomes all rain in the warm layer. The rain falls back into below freezing air, but since the depth is shallow, the rain does not have time to freeze into ice pellets (see Figure 14-4). The drops freeze on contact with the ground or exposed objects.

Figure 14-4. Freezing Rain Temperature Environment

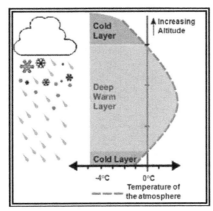

Rain occurs when there is a deep layer of above freezing air based at the surface (see Figure 14-5).

Figure 14-5. Rain Temperature Environment

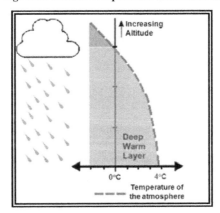

CHAPTER 15. ADVERSE WIND

15.1 Introduction. Adverse wind is a category of hazardous weather that is responsible for many weather-related accidents. Adverse winds include: crosswinds, gusts, tailwind, variable wind, and a sudden wind shift. Takeoff and landing are the most critical periods of any flight and are most susceptible to the effects of adverse wind. The most at-risk group is General Aviation (GA) pilots flying aircraft with lower crosswind and tailwind threshold values.

15.2 Crosswind. A crosswind is a wind that has a component directed perpendicularly to the heading of an aircraft. The potential of drift produced by crosswind is critical to air navigation, and can have its biggest impact during takeoff and landing. Airplanes take off and land more efficiently when oriented into the wind. The aircraft's groundspeed is minimized, a shorter runway is required to achieve lift-off, and the pilot has more time to make adjustments necessary for a smooth landing. As the wind turns more perpendicular to the runway to become a crosswind, the airplane directional control is affected. If a pilot does not correctly compensate for the crosswind, the aircraft may drift off the side of the runway or sideload on landing gear might occur. In extreme cases, the landing gear may collapse (see Figure 15-1 below).

Figure 15-1. Crosswind

15.3 Gust. A gust is a fluctuation of wind speed with variations of 10 knots or more between peaks and lulls.

Even if the airplane is oriented into the wind, gusts during takeoff and landing cause airspeed fluctuations which can cause problems for pilots. A gust increases airspeed, which increases lift, and may cause an aircraft to briefly balloon up. Once the gust ends, a sudden decrease of airspeed occurs, which decreases lift and causes the aircraft to sink. Gusty winds at the point of touchdown provide significant challenges to a safe landing.

15.4 **Tailwind.** A tailwind is a wind with a component of motion from behind the aircraft.

A tailwind can be hazardous during both takeoff and landing. A longer takeoff roll is necessary because a higher groundspeed is required to generate sufficient lift, and the aircraft may roll off the end of the runway before lift-off. Also, a smaller initial climb gradient occurs during takeoff, which may be insufficient to clear obstacles at the end of the runway. During a landing, a longer landing roll is required because the aircraft will touch down at a higher groundspeed. Wind should always be considered in takeoff performance planning.

15.5 **Variable Wind/Sudden Wind Shift.** A variable wind is a wind that changes direction frequently, while a sudden wind shift is a line or narrow zone along which there is an abrupt change of wind direction. Both, even at low wind speeds, can make takeoffs and landings difficult. A headwind can quickly become a crosswind or tailwind.

15.6 **Wind Shear.** Wind shear is the change in wind speed and/or direction, usually in the vertical. The characteristics of the wind shear profile are of critical importance in determining the impact for an aircraft on takeoff or landing.

Please refer to the current edition of AC 00-54, Pilot Windshear Guide, for additional information.

CHAPTER 16. WEATHER, OBSTRUCTIONS TO VISIBILITY, LOW CEILING, AND MOUNTAIN OBSCURATION

16.1 Weather and Obstructions to Visibility. Weather and obstructions to visibility include: fog, mist, haze, smoke, precipitation, blowing snow, dust storm, sandstorm, and volcanic ash.

16.1.1 Fog. Fog is a visible aggregate of minute water droplets that are based at the Earth's surface and reduces horizontal visibility to less than 5/8 statute mile (1 kilometer); unlike drizzle, it does not fall to the ground. Fog differs from cloud only in that its base must be at the Earth's surface, while clouds are above the surface.

Cloud droplets can remain liquid even when the air temperature is below freezing. Fog composed of water droplets and occurring with temperatures at or below freezing is termed freezing fog. When fog is composed of ice crystals, it is termed ice fog. If fog is so shallow that it is not an obstruction to vision at a height of 6 feet (2 meters) above the surface, it is called simply shallow (ground) fog.

Fog forms when the temperature and dewpoint of the air become identical (or nearly so). This may occur through cooling of the air to a little beyond its dewpoint (producing radiation fog, advection fog, or upslope fog), or by adding moisture and thereby elevating the dewpoint (producing frontal fog or steam fog). Fog seldom forms when the temperature-dewpoint spread is greater than 2 °C (4 °F).

16.1.1.1 Fog Types. Fog types are named according to their formation mechanism.

16.1.1.1.1 Radiation Fog. Radiation fog (see Figure 16-1) is a common type of fog, produced over a land area when radiational cooling reduces the air temperature to or below its dewpoint. Thus, radiation fog is generally a nighttime occurrence and often does not dissipate until after sunrise.

Figure 16-1. Radiation Fog

Radiation fog is relatively shallow fog. It may be dense enough to hide the entire sky or may conceal only part of the sky. Ground fog is a form of radiation fog that is confined to near ground level.

Factors favoring the formation of radiation fog are: 1) a shallow surface layer of relatively moist air beneath a dry layer, 2) clear skies, and 3) light surface winds. Terrestrial radiation cools the ground; in turn, the ground cools the air in contact with it. When the air is cooled to its dewpoint, fog forms. When rain soaks the ground, followed by clearing skies, radiation fog is not uncommon the following morning.

Radiation fog is restricted to land because water surfaces cool little from nighttime radiation. It is shallow when wind is calm. Winds up to about 5 knots mix the air slightly and tend to deepen the fog by spreading the cooling through a deeper layer. Stronger winds disperse the fog or mix the air through a still deeper layer with stratus clouds forming at the top of the mixing layer.

Ground fog usually burns off rather rapidly after sunrise. Other radiation fog generally clears before noon unless clouds move in over the fog. It can be difficult at times to differentiate between this and other types of fog, especially since nighttime cooling intensifies all fogs.

16.1.1.1.2 <u>Advection Fog</u>. Advection fog (see Figure 16-2) forms when moist air moves over a colder surface (see Figure 16-3), and the subsequent cooling of that air to below its dewpoint. It is most common along coastal areas, but often moves deep in continental areas. At sea, it is called sea fog. Advection fog deepens as wind speed increases up to about 15 knots. Wind much stronger than 15 knots lifts the fog into a layer of low stratus or stratocumulus clouds.

Figure 16-2. Advection Fog

Figure 16-3. Advection Fog Formation

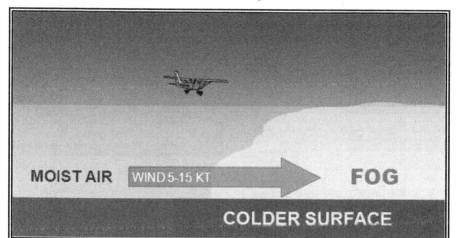

The west coast of the United States is quite vulnerable to advection fog. This fog frequently forms offshore as a result of cold water and then is carried inland by the wind. It can remain over the water for weeks, advancing over the land during night and retreating back over the water the next morning.

During the winter, advection fog over the central and eastern United States results when moist air from the Gulf of Mexico spreads northward over cold ground. The fog may extend as far north as the Great Lakes. Water areas in northern latitudes have frequent dense sea fog in summer as a result of warm, moist, tropical air flowing northward over colder Arctic waters.

A pilot will notice little difference between flying over advection fog and over radiation fog. Also, advection fog is usually more extensive and much more persistent than radiation fog. Advection fog can move in rapidly regardless of the time of day or night.

16.1.1.1.3 Upslope Fog. Upslope fog forms as a result of moist, stable air being adiabatically cooled to or below its dewpoint as it moves up sloping terrain. Winds speeds of 5 to 15 knots are most favorable since stronger winds tend to lift the fog into a layer of low stratus clouds. Unlike radiation fog, it can form under cloudy skies. Upslope fog is common along the eastern slopes of the Rockies, and somewhat less frequent east of the Appalachians. Upslope fog is often quite dense and extends to high altitudes.

16.1.1.1.4 Frontal Fog. When warm, moist air is lifted over a front, clouds and precipitation may form. If the cold air below is near its dewpoint, evaporation (or sublimation) from the precipitation may saturate the cold air and form fog (see Figure 16-4). A fog formed in this manner is called frontal (or precipitation-induced) fog. The result is a more or less continuous zone of condensed water droplets reaching from the ground up through the clouds. Frontal fog can become quite dense and continue for an extended period of time. This fog may extend over large areas, completely suspending air operations. It is most commonly associated with warm fronts, but can occur with other fronts as well.

Figure 16-4. Frontal Fog Formation

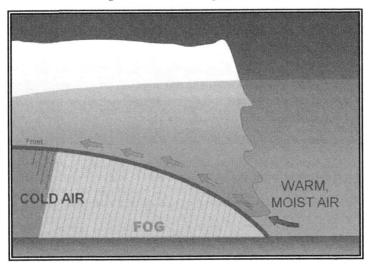

16.1.1.1.5 <u>Steam Fog</u>. When very cold air moves across relatively warm water, enough moisture may evaporate from the water surface to produce saturation. As the rising water vapor meets the cold air, it immediately recondenses and rises with the air that is being warmed from below. Because the air is destabilized, fog appears as rising filaments or streamers that resemble steam. This phenomenon is called steam fog. It is commonly observed over lakes and streams on cold autumn mornings, and over the ocean during the winter when cold air masses move off the continents and ice shelves. Steam fog is often very shallow, for as the steam rises, it reevaporates in the unsaturated air above. However, it can be dense and extend over large areas.

Steam fog is associated with a shallow layer of unstable air. Thus, pilots can expect convective turbulence flying through it. On occasion, columns of condensed vapor rise from the fog layer, forming whirling steam devils, which appear similar to the dust devils on land.

16.1.2 Mist. Mist is a visible aggregate of minute water droplets or ice crystals suspended in the atmosphere that reduces visibility to less than 7 statute miles (11 kilometers), but greater than, or equal to, 5/8 statute mile (1 kilometer). Mist forms a thin grayish veil that covers the landscape. It is similar to fog, but does not obstruct visibility to the same extent.

Mist may be considered an intermediate between fog and haze. It has lower relative humidity (95-99 percent) than fog and does not obstruct visibility to the same extent. However, there is no distinct line between any of these categories.

16.1.3 Haze. Haze is a suspension in the air of extremely small particles invisible to the naked eye and sufficiently numerous to give the air an opalescent appearance. It reduces visibility by scattering the shorter wavelengths of light. Haze produces a bluish color when viewed against a dark background and a yellowish veil when viewed against a light background. Haze may be distinguished by this same effect from mist, which yields only a gray obscuration. Certain haze particles increase in size with increasing relative humidity, drastically decreasing visibility. While visibility is a measure of how far one can see, including the ability to see the textures and colors therein, haze is the inability to view a similar scene with equal clarity.

Haze occurs in stable air and is usually only a few thousand feet thick, but may extend upwards to 15,000 feet (4,600 meters). A haze layer has a definite ceiling above which in-flight (air-to-air) visibility is unrestricted. At or below this level, the slant range (air-to-ground) visibility is poor. Visibility in haze varies greatly, depending on whether the pilot is facing into or away from the sun.

16.1.4 Smoke. Smoke is a suspension in the air of small particles produced by combustion due to fires, industrial burning, or other sources. It may transition to haze when the particles travel 25-100 miles (40-160 kilometers) or more, and the larger particles have settled and others become widely scattered through the atmosphere.

Not only can smoke reduce visibility to zero, many of its compounds are highly toxic and/or irritating. The most dangerous is carbon monoxide, which can lead to carbon monoxide poisoning, sometimes with supporting effects of hydrogen cyanide and phosgene.

When skies are clear above a surface-based layer of haze or smoke, visibility generally improves during the day. Heating during the day may cause convective mixing, spreading the smoke or haze to a higher altitude, and decreasing the concentration near the surface. However, the improvement is slower than the clearing of fog. Fog evaporates, but haze and smoke must be dispersed by the movement of air. A thick layer of clouds above haze or smoke may block sunlight, preventing dissipation. Visibility will improve little, if any, during the day.

16.1.5 Precipitation. Precipitation is any of the forms of water particles, whether liquid or solid, that fall from the atmosphere and reach the ground. Snow, rain, and drizzle are types of precipitation. Heavy snow may reduce visibility to zero. Rain seldom reduces surface visibility below 1 mile except in brief, heavy showers.

Drizzle usually restricts visibility to a greater degree than rain. It forms in stable air, falls from stratiform clouds, and is typically accompanied by fog. When drizzle changes to light rain, visibility usually improves because the droplet size increases, meaning there are fewer droplets per unit area.

16.1.6 Blowing Snow. Blowing snow is snow lifted from the surface of the Earth by the wind to a height of 6 feet (2 meters) or more above the ground, and blown about in such quantities that the reported horizontal visibility is reduced to less than 7 statute miles (11 kilometers). Light, dry powder snow is most prone to being blown by the wind. Strong winds keep the snow suspended up to 50 feet (15 meters) or so, obscuring the sky, and reducing surface visibility to near zero (called a whiteout). Visibility improves rapidly when the wind subsides.

16.1.7 Dust Storm. A dust storm is a severe weather condition characterized by strong winds and dust-filled air over an extensive area. Dust storms originate over regions when fine-grained soils, rich in clay and silt, are exposed to strong winds and lofted airborne. Fine-grained soils are commonly found in dry lake beds (called playas), river flood plains, ocean sediments, and glacial deposits.

Most of the dust originates from a number of discrete point sources. Intense dust storms reduce visibility to near zero in and near source regions, with visibility improving away from the source.

A dust storm is favored with extreme daytime heating of barren ground and a turbulent, unstable air mass that allows the dust to be lofted. Surface winds need to be 15 knots or greater to mobilize dust. A speed of 35 knots may be required over a desert surface that is covered with closely packed rock fragments called desert pavement. The average height of a dust storm is 3,000 to 6,000 feet (~1 kilometer). However, they can frequently extend up to 15,000 feet (4,600 meters).

Strong cooling after sunset quickly stabilizes the lowest atmosphere, forming a temperature inversion and settling the dust. Without turbulence, dust generally settles at a rate of 1,000 feet (300 meters) per hour. It can take many hours (or days) for the dust to settle. However, precipitation will very effectively remove dust from the atmosphere.

Aircraft operation in a dust storm can be very hazardous. Visibility can drop to zero in a matter of seconds. Dust can also clog the air intake of engines, damage electro-optical systems, and cause problems with human health.

From a pilot's point of view, it is important to recognize that slant range (air-to-ground) visibility in dust is generally reduced compared to reported surface (horizontal) visibility. Therefore, it may not be possible to pick out an airfield from above, even when reported surface visibility is three miles or more.

16.1.8 Sandstorm. A sandstorm is particles of sand carried aloft by a strong wind. The sand particles are mostly confined to the lowest 10 feet (3.5 meters), and rarely rise more than 50 feet (15 meters) above the ground. Sandstorms are similar to dust storms, but occur on a localized scale. This is because sand particles are larger and heavier than dust particles. Sandstorms are best developed in desert regions where there is loose sand, often in dunes, without much admixture of dust.

16.1.8.1   Haboob. A haboob (see Figure 16-5) is a dust storm or sandstorm that forms as cold downdrafts from a thunderstorm turbulently lift dust and sand into the air. While haboobs are often short-lived, they can be quite intense. The dust wall may extend horizontally for more than 60 miles (100 kilometers) and rise vertically to the base of the thunderstorm. Spinning whirlwinds of dust frequently form along the turbulent cold air outflow, giving rise to huge dust/sand whirls.

Figure 16-5. Haboob

16.1.9 <u>Volcanic Ash</u>. Volcanic ash is made up of fine particles of rock powder that originate from a volcano and that may remain suspended in the atmosphere for long periods. Severe volcanic eruptions that send ash into the upper atmosphere occur somewhere around the world several times per year. The ash plume may not be visible, especially at night or in instrument meteorological conditions (IMC). Even if visible, it is difficult to distinguish visually between an ash cloud and an ordinary cloud. Ash cannot be detected by air traffic control (ATC) radar. However, it may be detected by weather radar, particularly during the early stages of a volcanic eruption when the ash is more concentrated.

Flying into a volcanic ash cloud can be exceedingly dangerous. Volcanic ash is composed of silica (glass). When ash is ingested into a jet engine, it melts to produce a soft sticky molten product that adheres to the compressor turbine blades and fuel injectors/igniters. With no air going into the engine, the fuel cannot ignite, the engine comes to a slow spinning stop by spooling down, and a flameout occurs. As the aircraft exits the ash cloud and into colder temperatures, the cooled, hardened silicas on the turbine blades become dislodged, allowing the fan blades to start rotating, and allow for an engine relight as the air starts moving through the engine again. Piston-powered aircraft are less likely to lose power, but severe damage is almost certain to ensue after an encounter with a volcanic ash cloud that is only a few hours old.

Volcanic ash also causes abrasive damage to aircraft flying through it at hundreds of miles per hour. Particles impacting the windshield can sandblast the surface into a frosted finish that obscures the pilot's view. The sandblasting can also remove paint and pit metal on the nose and leading edges of wings and navigation equipment. Ash contaminates aircraft ventilation, hydraulic, instrument, electronic, and air data systems. Ash covering a runway can cover its markings and cause aircraft to lose traction during takeoffs and landings.

16.2 Low Ceiling and Mountain Obscuration.

16.2.1 Low Ceiling. Stratus is the most frequent cloud associated with low ceilings. Stratus clouds, like fog, are composed of extremely small water droplets or ice crystals suspended in air. An observer on a mountain in a stratus layer would call it fog. Stratus and fog frequently exist together. In many cases, there is no real line of distinction between the fog and stratus; rather, one gradually merges into the other. Flight visibility may approach zero in stratus clouds. Stratus over land tends to be lowest during night and early morning, lifting or dissipating due to solar heating by late morning or early afternoon. Low stratus clouds often occur when moist air mixes with a colder air mass, or in any situation where temperature-dewpoint spread is small.

Not all ceilings are equally hazardous to a pilot. An indefinite ceiling is more hazardous than an equal ceiling caused by a layer aloft. Once a pilot descends below a ceiling caused by a layer aloft, the pilot can see both the ground below and the runway ahead. However, an indefinite ceiling restricts the pilot's slant range (air-to-ground) visibility. Thus, the pilot may not see the runway ahead after he descends below the indefinite ceiling (see Figure 16-6).

Figure 16-6. Layer Aloft Ceiling Versus Indefinite Ceiling

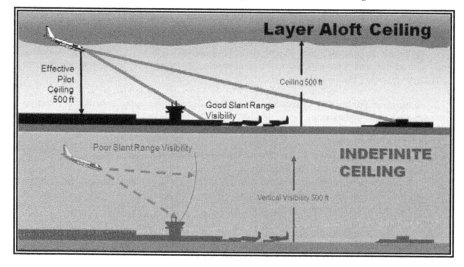

16.2.2 <u>Mountain Obscuration</u>. A mountain obscuration is a condition in which mountains or mountain ridges are obscured due to clouds, precipitation, smoke, or other obscurations.

Flight can be especially hazardous over mountain routes when the mountains are obscured. The large elevation variations around mountains can cause surface weather observations to mislead. For example, a weather station located in a valley could report a visual flight rules (VFR) cloud ceiling, while a hiker in the mountains sees fog.

CHAPTER 17. TURBULENCE

17.1 Introduction. Aircraft turbulence is irregular motion of an aircraft in flight, especially when characterized by rapid up-and-down motion caused by a rapid variation of atmospheric wind velocities. Turbulence varies from annoying bumpiness to severe jolts which cause structural damage to aircraft and/or injury to its passengers. Turbulence intensities and their associated aircraft reactions are described in the Aeronautical Information Manual (AIM).

17.2 Causes of Turbulence. Turbulence is caused by convective currents (called convective turbulence), obstructions in the wind flow (called mechanical turbulence), and wind shear.

17.2.1 <u>Convective Turbulence</u>. Convective turbulence is turbulent vertical motions that result from convective currents and the subsequent rising and sinking of air. For every rising current, there is a compensating downward current. The downward currents frequently occur over broader areas than do the upward currents; therefore, they have a slower vertical speed than do the rising currents.

Convective currents are most active on warm summer afternoons when winds are light. Heated air at the surface creates a shallow, absolutely unstable layer within which bubbles of warm air rise upward. Convection increases in strength and to greater heights as surface heating increases. Barren surfaces such as sandy or rocky wastelands and plowed fields become hotter than open water or ground covered by vegetation. Thus, air at and near the surface heats unevenly. Because of uneven heating, the strength of convective currents can vary considerably within short distances.

As air moves upward, it cools by expansion. A convective current continues upward until it reaches a level where its temperature cools to the same as that of the surrounding air. If it cools to saturation, a cumuliform cloud forms.

Billowy cumuliform clouds, usually seen over land during sunny afternoons, are signposts in the sky indicating convective turbulence. The cloud top usually marks the approximate upper limit of the convective current. A pilot can expect to encounter turbulence beneath or in the clouds, while above the clouds, air generally is smooth (see Figure 17-1). When convection extends to great heights, it develops larger towering cumulus clouds and cumulonimbus with anvil-like tops. The cumulonimbus gives visual warning of violent convective turbulence.

Figure 17-1. Convective Turbulence

When the air is too dry for cumuliform clouds to form, convective currents can still be active. This is called dry convection, or thermals (see Figure 17-2). A pilot has little or no indication of their presence until encountering the turbulence.

Figure 17-2. Thermals

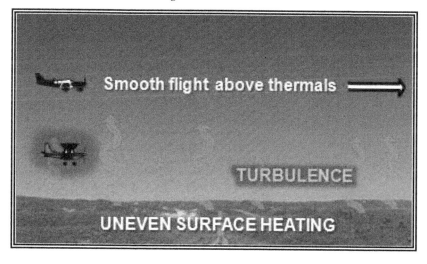

17.2.2 Mechanical Turbulence. Mechanical turbulence is turbulence caused by obstructions to the wind flow, such as trees, buildings, mountains, and so on. Obstructions to the wind flow disrupt smooth wind flow into a complex snarl of eddies (see Figure 17-3). An aircraft flying through these eddies experiences mechanical turbulence.

Figure 17-3. Mechanical Turbulence

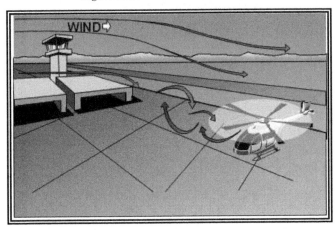

The intensity of mechanical turbulence depends on wind speed and roughness of the obstructions. The higher the speed and/or the rougher the surface, the greater the turbulence.

The wind carries the turbulent eddies downstream. How far depends on wind speed and stability of the air. Unstable air allows larger eddies to form than those that form in stable air; but the instability breaks up the eddies quickly, while in stable air they dissipate slowly.

17.2.2.1 **Mountain Waves.** A mountain wave (see Figure 17-4) is an atmospheric wave disturbance formed when stable air flow passes over a mountain or mountain ridge. Mountain waves are a form of mechanical turbulence which develop above and downwind of mountains. The waves remain nearly stationary while the wind blows rapidly through them. The waves may extend 600 miles (1,000 kilometers) or more downwind from the mountain range. Mountain waves frequently produce severe to extreme turbulence. Location and intensity varies with wave characteristics. Incredibly, vertically propagating mountain waves have been documented up to 200,000 feet (60,000 meters) and higher.

Figure 17-4. Mountain Waves

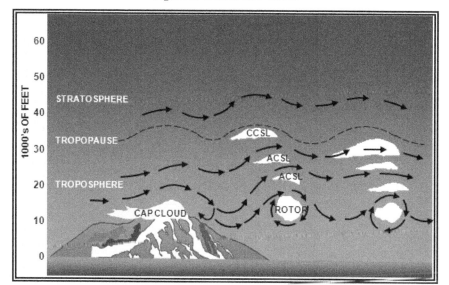

Mountain waves often produce violent downdrafts on the immediate leeward side of the mountain barrier. Sometimes the downward speed exceeds the maximum climb rate of an aircraft and may drive the aircraft into the mountainside.

A mountain wave cloud is a cloud that forms in the rising branches of mountain waves and occupies the crests of the waves. The most distinctive are the sharp-edged, lens-, or almond-shaped lenticular clouds. When sufficient moisture is present in the upstream flow, mountain waves produce interesting cloud formations (see Figure 17-5) including: cap clouds, cirrocumulus standing lenticular (CCSL), Altocumulus Standing Lenticular (ACSL), and rotor clouds. These clouds provide visual proof that mountain waves exist. However, these clouds may be absent if the air is too dry.

For additional information on hazardous mountain waves, refer to the current edition of AC 00-57, Hazardous Mountain Winds and their Visual Indicators.

Figure 17-5. Mountain Wave Clouds

17.2.3 <u>Wind Shear Turbulence</u>. Wind shear is the rate of change in wind direction and/or speed per unit distance. Wind shear generates turbulence between two wind currents of different directions and/or speeds (see Figure 17-6). Wind shear may be associated with either a wind shift or a wind speed gradient at any level in the atmosphere.

Figure 17-6. Wind Shear Turbulence

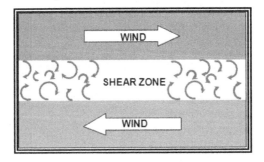

17.2.3.1 Temperature Inversion. A temperature inversion is a layer of the atmosphere in which temperature increases with altitude. Inversions commonly occur within the lowest few thousand feet above ground due to nighttime radiational cooling, along frontal zones, and when cold air is trapped in a valley. Strong wind shears often occur across temperature inversion layers, which can generate turbulence (see Figure 17-7).

Figure 17-7. Wind Shear Turbulence Associated with a Temperature Inversion

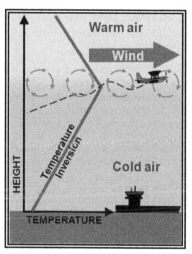

17.2.3.2 Clear Air Turbulence (CAT). Clear Air Turbulence (CAT) is a higher altitude (~20,000 to 50,000 feet) turbulence phenomenon occurring in cloud-free regions associated with wind shear, particularly between the core of a jet stream and the surrounding air. It can often affect an aircraft without warning. CAT frequency and intensity are maximized during winter when jet streams are strongest.

For additional information on CAT, refer to the current edition of AC 00-30, Clear Air Turbulence Avoidance.

17.3 Turbulence Factors. How an aircraft will respond to turbulence varies with: intensity of the turbulence, aircraft size, wing loading, airspeed, and aircraft altitude. When an aircraft travels rapidly from one current to another, it undergoes abrupt changes in acceleration.

CHAPTER 18. ICING

18.1 **Introduction.** In general, icing is any deposit of ice forming on an object. It is one of the major weather hazards to aviation. Icing is a cumulative hazard. The longer an aircraft collects icing, the worse the hazard becomes.

18.2 **Supercooled Water.** Freezing is a complex process. Pure water suspended in the air does not freeze until it reaches a temperature of -40 °C. This occurs because surface tension of the droplets inhibits freezing. The smaller and purer the water droplet, the more likely it is supercooled. Also, supercooled water can exist as large drops known as Supercooled Large Drops (SLD). SLDs are common in freezing rain and freezing drizzle situations (see paragraph 18.3.2.1).

Supercooled water content of clouds varies with temperature. Between 0 and -10 °C clouds consist mainly of supercooled water droplets. Between -10 and -20 °C, liquid droplets coexist with ice crystals. Below -20 °C, clouds are generally composed entirely of ice crystals. However, strong vertical currents (e.g., cumulonimbus) may carry supercooled water to great heights where temperatures are as low as -40 °C.

Supercooled water will readily freeze if sufficiently agitated. This explains why airplanes collect ice when they pass through a liquid cloud or precipitation composed of supercooled droplets.

18.3 **Structural Icing.** Structural icing is the stuff that sticks to the outside of the airplane. It occurs when supercooled water droplets strike the airframe and freeze. Structural icing can be categorized into three types: rime, clear (or glaze), and mixed.

Icing intensities are described in the Aeronautical Information Manual (AIM).

18.3.1 Rime Icing. Rime ice is rough, milky, and opaque ice formed by the instantaneous freezing of small, supercooled water droplets after they strike the aircraft. It is the most frequently reported icing type. Rime ice can pose a hazard because its jagged texture can disrupt an aircraft's aerodynamic integrity.

Rime icing formation favors colder temperatures, lower liquid water content, and small droplets. It grows when droplets rapidly freeze upon striking an aircraft. The rapid freezing traps air and forms a porous, brittle, opaque, and milky-colored ice. Rime ice grows into the air stream from the forward edges of wings and other exposed parts of the airframe.

18.3.2 Clear Icing. Clear ice (or glaze ice) is a glossy, clear, or translucent ice formed by the relatively slow freezing of large, supercooled water droplets. Clear icing conditions exist more often in an environment with warmer temperatures, higher liquid water contents, and larger droplets.

Clear ice forms when only a small portion of the drop freezes immediately while the remaining unfrozen portion flows or smears over the aircraft surface and gradually freezes. Few air bubbles are trapped during this gradual process. Thus, clear ice is less opaque and denser than rime ice. It can appear either as a thin smooth surface, or as rivulets, streaks, or bumps on the aircraft.

Clear icing is a more hazardous ice type for many reasons. It tends to form horns near the top and bottom of the airfoils leading edge, which greatly affects airflow. This results in an area of disrupted and turbulent airflow that is considerably larger than that caused by rime ice. Since it is clear and difficult to see, the pilot may not be able to quickly recognize that it is occurring. It can be difficult to remove since it can spread beyond the deicing or anti-icing equipment, although in most cases it is removed nearly completely by deicing devices.

18.3.2.1   Supercooled Large Drops (SLD). A type of clear icing that is especially dangerous to flight operations is ice formed from SLDs. These are water droplets in a subfreezing environment with diameters larger than 40 microns, such as freezing drizzle (40 to 200 microns) and freezing rain (>200 microns). These larger droplets can flow along the airfoil for some distance prior to freezing. SLDs tend to form a very lumpy, uneven, and textured ice similar to glass in a bathroom window.

SLD ice tends to form aft, beyond the reach of deicing equipment. Thus, ice remaining on the airfoil continues to disrupt the airflow and reduce the aircraft's aerodynamic integrity. Even a small amount of ice on the lower and upper surfaces of the airfoil can seriously disrupt its aerodynamic properties. The residual ice generates turbulence along a significant portion of the airfoil. This residual ice can act as a spoiler, a device actually used to slow an aircraft in flight. In extreme cases, turbulence and flow separation bubbles can travel along the airfoil and inadvertently activate the ailerons, creating dangerously unstable flying conditions.

18.3.3 Mixed Icing. Mixed ice is a mixture of clear ice and rime ice. It forms as an airplane collects both rime and clear ice due to small-scale (tens of kilometers or less) variations in liquid water content, temperature, and droplet sizes. Mixed ice appears as layers of relatively clear and opaque ice when examined from the side.

Mixed icing poses a similar hazard to an aircraft as clear ice. It may form horns or other shapes that disrupt airflow and cause handling and performance problems. It can spread over more of the airframe's surface and is more difficult to remove than rime ice. It can also spread over a portion of airfoil not protected by anti-icing or deicing equipment. Ice forming farther aft causes flow separation and turbulence over a large area of the airfoil, which decreases the ability of the airfoil to keep the aircraft in flight.

18.3.4 Icing Factors. Structural icing is determined by many factors. The meteorological quantities most closely related to icing type and severity are, in order of importance: Supercooled Liquid Water Content (SLWC), temperature (altitude), and droplet size. However, aircraft type/design and airspeed are also important factors.

SLWC is important in determining how much water is available for icing. The highest quantities can be found in cumuliform clouds with the lowest quantities in stratiform clouds. However, in most icing cases, SLWC is low.

Icing potential is very temperature dependent. For icing to occur, the outside air temperature must be below 0 °C. As clouds get colder, SLWC decreases until only ice crystals remain. Thus, almost all icing tends to occur in the temperature interval between 0 °C and -20 °C, with about half of all reports occurring between -8 °C and -12 °C. In altitude terms, the peak of occurrence is near 10,000 feet, with approximately half of incidents occurring between 5,000 feet and 13,000 feet. The only physical cold limit to icing is at -40 °C because liquid droplets freeze without nuclei present.

In general, rime icing tends to occur at temperatures colder than -15 °C, clear when the temperature is warmer than -10 °C, and mixed ice at temperatures in between. This is only general guidance. The type of icing will vary depending on the liquid water content, droplet size, and aircraft-specific variables.

An airframe can remain cold (temperature below 0 °C) in a warm (temperature above 0 °C) atmosphere if it is cold soaked. For example, if an aircraft has been flying in a cold environment, but then descends into warmer temperatures, the airframe does not heat up immediately to the air temperature. For some aircraft, the airframe can remain colder than 0 °C for some time, even after landing. Aircraft with fuel tanks flush-mounted to the airframe are particularly susceptible to icing, even in an environment where the air temperature is slightly above 0 °C. Because these characteristics vary from airframe to airframe, it is important for pilots to be aware of the limitations of their aircraft.

Droplet size can influence icing, but is not as important as SLWC and temperature, unless the droplets are larger than cloud droplets in size (e.g., freezing drizzle and freezing rain). Droplet size affects the collection of drops by the airframe. Small droplets tend to impact the airfoil near the plane's leading edge. Larger drops, including freezing rain and freezing drizzle, can cross the streamlines and impact farther back.

Aircraft airspeed is an important nonmeteorological factor which determines icing type and severity. The rate of supercooled water droplet impact increases with airspeed, which acts to increase ice accumulation, but this is counteracted by the increase of airframe skin surface heating due to friction. Typically, airframe icing is negligible at speeds above 575 knots.

Aircraft type and design are also important factors. Because these characteristics vary, it is important for pilots to be aware of the limitations of their aircraft.

Commercial jet aircraft are generally less vulnerable to structural icing than light turboprop aircraft. This is due to their rapid airspeed, powerful deicing equipment, and tendency to cruise at higher altitudes where temperatures are typically too cold for icing. Conversely, light turboprop aircraft are more susceptible to icing because they typically fly at lower altitudes where icing is more common and at slower speeds.

18.3.5 Icing in Stratiform Clouds. Icing in middle and low-level stratiform clouds is confined, on the average, to a layer between 3,000 and 4,000 feet thick. Thus, a change in altitude of only a few thousand feet may take the aircraft out of icing conditions, even if it remains in clouds. Icing intensity generally ranges from a trace to light, with the maximum values occurring in the cloud's upper portions. Both rime and mixed are found in stratiform clouds. The main hazard lies in the great horizontal extent of stratiform clouds layers. High-level stratiform clouds (i.e., at temperatures colder than -20 °C) are composed mostly of ice crystals and produce little icing.

18.3.6 Icing in Cumuliform Clouds. The icing layer in cumuliform clouds is smaller horizontally, but greater vertically than in stratiform clouds. Icing is more variable in cumuliform clouds because many of the factors conducive to icing depend on the particular cloud's stage of development. Icing intensities may range from a trace in small cumulus to severe in a large towering cumulus or cumulonimbus. Although icing occurs at all levels above the freezing level in a building cumuliform cloud, it is most intense in the upper portion of the cloud where the updraft is concentrated and SLDs are plentiful. Icing can extend to great heights in towering cumulus and cumulonimbus where strong updrafts allow SLDs to exist at temperatures as cold as -40 °C. Icing in a cumuliform cloud is usually clear or mixed with rime in the upper levels.

18.3.7 Icing with Fronts. Most icing reports occur in the vicinity of fronts. This icing can occur both above and below the front (see Figure 18-1).

For significant icing to occur above the front, the warm air must be lifted and cooled to saturation at temperatures below zero, making it contain supercooled water droplets. The supercooled water droplets freeze on impact with an aircraft. If the warm air is unstable, icing may be sporadic; if it is stable, icing may be continuous over an extended area. A line of showers or thunderstorms along a cold front may produce icing, but only in a comparatively narrow band along the front.

Figure 18-1. Icing with Fronts

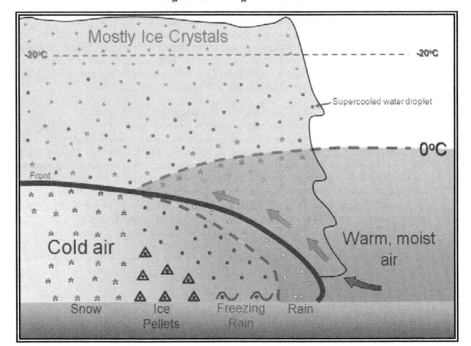

A favored location for severe clear icing is freezing rain and/or freezing drizzle below a front. Rain forms above the frontal surface at temperatures warmer than freezing. Subsequently, it falls through air at temperatures below freezing and becomes supercooled. The SLDs freeze on impact with an aircraft. If the below freezing layer is shallow, freezing rain will occur at the surface. If the below freezing layer is deep, the supercooled droplets may freeze into ice pellets. Ice pellets indicate icing above. The icing can be severe because of the large amount of supercooled water. Icing in freezing precipitation is especially dangerous because it often extends horizontally over a broad area and a pilot may be unable to escape it by descending to a lower altitude.

18.3.8 <u>Icing with Mountains</u>. Icing is more likely and more severe in mountainous regions. Mountain ranges cause upward air motions on their windward side. These vertical currents support large supercooled water droplets above the freezing level. The movement of a front across a mountain range combines frontal lift with the mountain's upslope flow effect to create extremely hazardous icing zones (see <u>Figure 18-2</u>).

Figure 18-2. Icing with Mountains

The most severe icing occurs above the crests and on the ridges' windward side. This zone usually extends to about 5,000 feet above the mountaintops, but can extend much higher if cumuliform clouds develop.

Icing with mountains can be especially hazardous because a pilot may be unable to descend to above freezing temperatures due to terrain elevation. If a pilot approaches a mountain ridge from the windward side, his aircraft may be unable to climb above the mountaintops, or even maintain altitude due to severe ice accumulation. The end result may be a crash.

18.3.9 <u>Icing Hazards</u>. Structural icing degrades an aircraft's performance. It destroys the smooth flow of air, increasing drag while decreasing the ability of the airfoil to create lift. The actual weight of ice on an airplane is insignificant when compared to the airflow disruption it causes. As power is added to compensate for the additional drag, and the nose is lifted to maintain altitude, the angle of attack is increased. This allows the underside of the wings and fuselage to accumulate additional ice.

Wind tunnel and flight tests have shown that frost, snow, and ice accumulations (on the leading edge or upper surface of the wing) no thicker or rougher than a piece of coarse sandpaper can reduce lift by 30 percent and increase drag up to 40 percent. Larger accretions can reduce lift even more and can increase drag by 80 percent or more.

Ice accumulates on every exposed frontal surface of the airplane: wings, propeller, windshield, antennas, vents, intakes, and cowlings. It can build in flight where no heat or boots can reach it. It can cause antennas to vibrate so severely that they break. In moderate to severe icing, a light aircraft could be subject to enough ice accumulation or accretion that continued flight is impossible. The airplane may stall at much higher speeds and lower angles of attack than normal. It can roll or pitch uncontrollably, and recovery might be impossible.

Regardless of anti-ice or deice protection offered by the aircraft, a pilot's first course of action should be to leave the area of visible moisture. This might mean descending to an altitude below the cloud bases, climbing to an altitude that is above the cloud tops, or turning to a different course. If this is not possible, then the pilot must move to an altitude where the temperature is above freezing.

18.4   Engine Icing.

18.4.1 Carburetor Icing. In an aspirated engine, the carburetion process can lower the temperature of the incoming air by as much as 33 °C. If the moisture content is high enough, ice will form on the throttle plate and venturi, gradually shutting off the supply of air to the engine. Even a small amount of carburetor ice will result in power loss and may make the engine run rough. It is possible for carburetor ice to form even when the skies are clear and the outside temperature is as high as 33 °C (90 °F) if the relative humidity is 50 percent or more.

18.4.2 High Ice Water Content (HIWC). High Ice Water Content (HIWC) is a relatively new icing hazard, at least from the standpoint of research and understanding. HIWC refers to high altitude ice crystals, which may exist in the tops and anvils of cumulonimbus clouds and thunderstorms. Under certain HIWC conditions, turbine engine performance can be affected, including flameouts. Research into HIWC conditions continues as of the writing of this section.

8/23/16   AC 00-6B

CHAPTER 19. THUNDERSTORMS

19.1 Introduction. A thunderstorm is a local storm, invariably produced by a cumulonimbus cloud, and always accompanied by lightning and thunder, usually with strong gusts of wind, heavy rain, and sometimes with hail. There are as many as 40,000 thunderstorm occurrences each day worldwide, and the United States certainly experiences its share. Thunderstorms are barriers to air traffic because they are usually too tall to fly over, too dangerous to fly through or under, and can be difficult to circumnavigate.

19.2 Necessary Ingredients for Thunderstorm Cell Formation. Thunderstorm cell formation requires three ingredients: sufficient water vapor, unstable air, and a lifting mechanism (see Figure 19-1). Sufficient water vapor (commonly measured using dewpoint) must be present to produce unstable air. Virtually all showers and thunderstorms form in an air mass that is classified as conditionally unstable. A conditionally unstable air mass requires a lifting mechanism strong enough to release the instability. Lifting mechanisms include: converging winds around surface lows and troughs, fronts, upslope flow, drylines, outflow boundaries generated by prior storms, and local winds, such as sea breeze, lake breeze, land breeze, and valley breeze circulations.

Figure 19-1. Necessary Ingredients for Thunderstorm Cell Formation

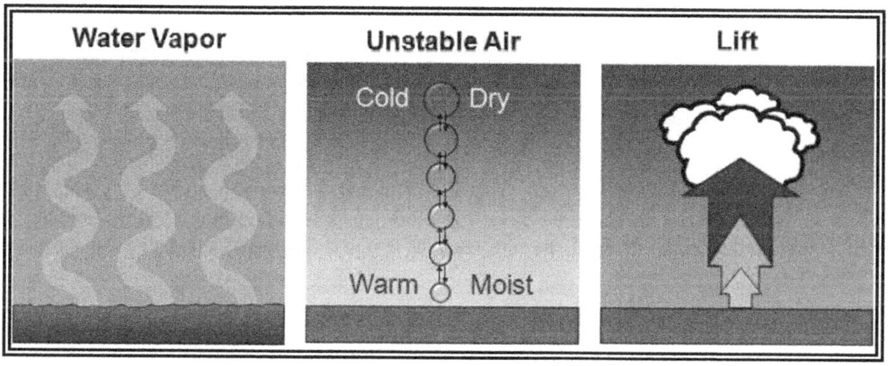

19.3 Thunderstorm Cell Life Cycle. A thunderstorm cell is the convective cell of a cumulonimbus cloud having lightning and thunder. It undergoes three distinct stages during its life cycle (see Figure 19-2): towering cumulus, mature, and dissipating. The total life cycle is typically about 30 minutes.

The distinguishing feature of the towering cumulus stage is a strong convective updraft. The updraft is a bubble of warm, rising air concentrated near the top of the cloud which leaves a cloudy trail in its wake. Updraft speeds can exceed 3,000 feet per minute.

Figure 19-2. Thunderstorm Cell Life Cycle

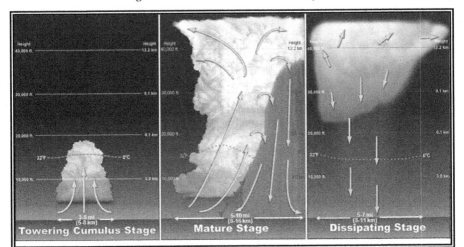

The cell transitions to the mature stage when precipitation reaches the surface. Precipitation descends through the cloud and drags the adjacent air downward, creating a strong downdraft alongside the updraft. The downdraft spreads out along the surface, well in advance of the parent thunderstorm cell, as a mass of cool, gusty air. The arc-shaped leading edge of downdraft air resembles a miniature cold front and is called a gust front. Uplift along the gust front may trigger the formation of new cells, sometimes well ahead of the parent cell. Cumulonimbus tops frequently penetrate into the lower stratosphere as an overshooting top, where strong winds aloft distort the cloud top into an anvil shape. Weather hazards reach peak intensity toward the end of the mature stage.

The dissipating stage is marked by a strong downdraft embedded within the area of precipitation. Subsiding air replaces the updraft throughout the cloud, effectively cutting off the supply of moisture provided by the updraft. Precipitation tapers off and ends. Compression warms the subsiding air and the relative humidity drops. The convective cloud gradually vaporizes from below, leaving only a remnant anvil cloud.

19.4   Thunderstorm Types. There are three principal thunderstorm types: single cell, multicell (cluster and line), and supercell. All thunderstorms are hazardous to aircraft.

A single cell (also called ordinary cell) thunderstorm consists of only one cell. Its life cycle was covered in the previous section. It is easily circumnavigated by pilots, except at night or when embedded in other clouds. Single cell thunderstorms are rare; almost all thunderstorms are multicell.

A multicell cluster thunderstorm (see Figure 19-3 and Figure 19-4) consists of a cluster of cells at various stages of their life cycle. With an organized multicell cluster, as the first cell matures, it is carried downwind, and a new cell forms upwind to take its place. A multicell cluster may have a lifetime of several hours (or more). New cells will continue to form as long as the three necessary ingredients exist (see paragraph 19.2). Its size and persistence make it a bit tougher to circumnavigate than a single cell thunderstorm. An area of multicell cluster thunderstorms can be like a mine field for air traffic.

Figure 19-3. Multicell Cluster Thunderstorm

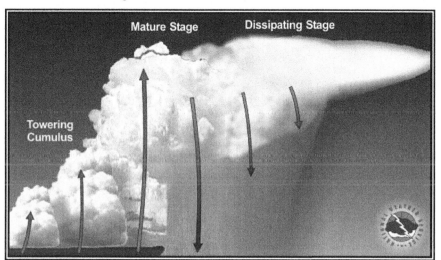

Sometimes thunderstorms will form in a line that can extend laterally for hundreds of miles. New cells continually re-form at the leading edge of the system with rain, and sometimes hail, following behind. Sometimes storms which comprise the line can be supercells. The line can persist for many hours (or more) as long as the three necessary ingredients continue to exist. These squall lines are the thunderstorm type which presents the most effective barrier to air traffic because the line is usually too tall to fly over, too dangerous to fly through or under, and difficult to circumnavigate. About 25 percent of all U.S. tornadoes are spawned by squall lines.

Figure 19-4. Multicell Line Thunderstorm

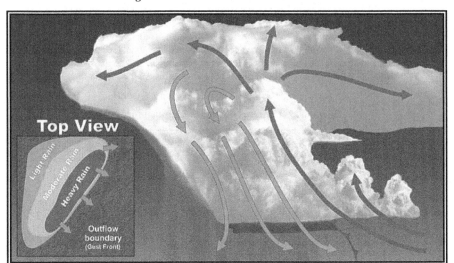

A supercell thunderstorm (see Figure 19-5) is an often dangerous convective storm that consists primarily of a single, quasi-steady rotating updraft that persists for an extended period of time. It has a very organized internal structure that enables it to produce especially dangerous weather for pilots who encounter them. Updraft speeds may reach 9,000 feet per minute (100 knots). This allows hazards to be magnified to an even greater degree. Nearly all supercells produce severe weather (e.g., large hail or damaging wind) and about 25 percent produce a tornado. A supercell may persist for many hours (or longer). New cells will continue to form as long as the three necessary ingredients exist (see paragraph 19.2).

A supercell's size and persistence make it a bit tougher to circumnavigate than a single cell thunderstorm. Also, multicell clusters and lines may have supercells incorporated as part of the system as well.

Figure 19-5. Supercell Thunderstorm

19.5 Factors that Influence Thunderstorm Motion. A thunderstorm is a process, not a solid object or block of wood. Storm motion equals the combined effects of both advection and propagation (see Figure 19-6). Advection is the component of storm motion due to individual cells moving with the average wind throughout the vertical depth of the cumulonimbus cloud. The wind at FL180 (500 millibars) usually provides a good approximation. Propagation is the component of storm motion due to old cell dissipation and the new cell development. Storm motion may deviate substantially from the motion of the individual cells which comprise the storm.

Figure 19-6. Factors that Influence Thunderstorm Motion

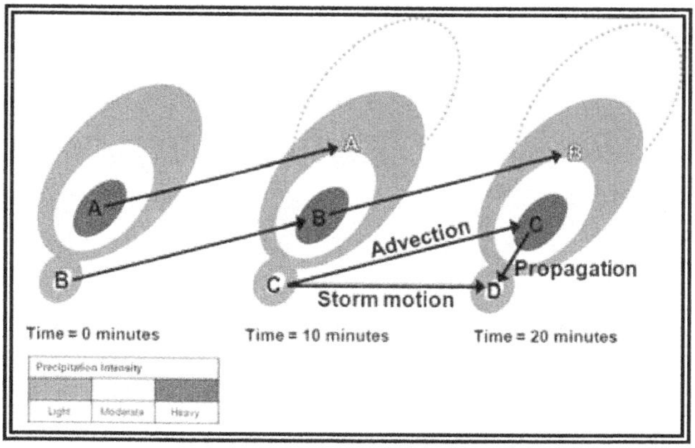

Individual cells which comprise the storm move northeast (advection), but dissipate and are replaced by new cells (propagation). Storm motion equals the combined effects of both advection and propagation.

19.6 Hazards. A thunderstorm can pack just about every aviation weather hazard into one vicious bundle. These hazards include: lightning, adverse winds, downbursts, turbulence, icing, hail, rapid altimeter changes, static electricity, and tornadoes.

19.6.1 Lightning. Every thunderstorm produces lightning and thunder by definition. Lightning is a visible electrical discharge produced by a thunderstorm. The discharge may occur within or between clouds, between the cloud and air, between a cloud and the ground, or between the ground and a cloud.

Lightning can damage or disable an aircraft. It can puncture the skin of an aircraft. It can damage communication and electronic navigational equipment. Nearby lightning can blind the pilot, rendering him or her momentarily unable to navigate either by instrument or by visual reference. Nearby lightning can also induce permanent errors in the magnetic compass. Lightning discharges, even distant ones, can disrupt radio communications on low and medium frequencies. Lightning has been suspected of igniting fuel vapors, causing explosion; however, serious accidents due to lightning strikes are extremely rare.

19.6.2 Adverse Wind. Adverse winds are always found within thunderstorms and often many miles away from the precipitation area. Crosswinds, gusts, and variable winds/sudden wind shifts can lead to a crash during takeoffs, approaches, and landings. The area along and immediately behind the gust front is particularly dangerous because this is where rapid and sometimes drastic changes in surface winds occur.

19.6.3 Downburst. Shower and thunderstorm cells sometimes produce intense downdrafts called downbursts that create strong, often damaging winds. Downbursts (see Figure 19-7) can create hazardous conditions for pilots and have been responsible for many low-level wind shear accidents. Smaller, shorter-lived downbursts are called microbursts.

A downburst is especially dangerous to airplanes when it is encountered when climbing from takeoff or approaching to land. During this phase, the aircraft is operating at relatively slow speeds. A major change of wind velocity can lead to loss of lift and a crash.

Figure 19-7. Downburst Life Cycle

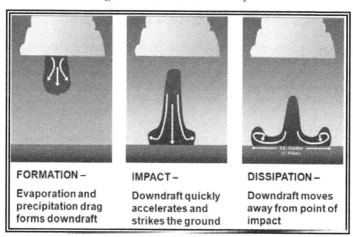

A microburst is particularly dangerous during landing if the pilot has reduced power and lowered the nose in response to the headwind shear (see Figure 19-8). This leaves the aircraft in a nose-low, power-low configuration when the tailwind shear occurs, which makes recovery more difficult. It can cause the airplane to stall or land short of the runway.

Figure 19-8. Landing in a Microburst

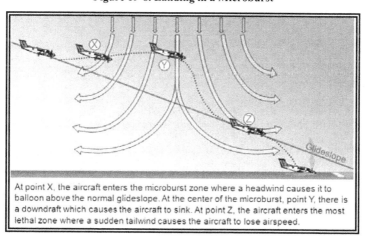

Pilots should be alert for indications of a microburst early in the approach phase, and ready to initiate a missed approach at the first indication. However, it may be impossible to recover from a microburst encounter at low altitude.

19.6.4 Turbulence. Turbulence is present in all thunderstorms. Severe or extreme turbulence is common. Gust loads can be severe enough to stall an aircraft at maneuvering speed or to cause structural damage at cruising speed. The strongest turbulence occurs with shear between updrafts and downdrafts. Outside the cumulonimbus cloud, turbulence has been encountered several thousand feet above, and 20 miles laterally from, a severe storm.

The wind-shear zone between the gust front and surrounding air is very turbulent airspace. Oftentimes, the surface position of the gust front is denoted by a line of dust or debris along the ground, or a line of spray along bodies of water. Sometimes the gust front shear zone is denoted by a shelf cloud (see Figure 19-9), which forms as warm, moist air is lifted by the gust front. Shelf clouds are most common with multicell line thunderstorms.

Figure 19-9. Thunderstorm with Shelf Cloud

19.6.5 Icing. Thunderstorms produce abundant supercooled liquid water above the freezing level. When temperature in the upward current cools to about -15 °C, much of the remaining water vapor sublimates as ice crystals; and above this level, the amount of supercooled water decreases. However, supercooled water can exist at temperatures as cold as -40 °C in the presence of vigorous upward vertical motion, such as in a thunderstorm updraft.

Supercooled water freezes on impact with an aircraft. Clear icing can occur at any altitude above the freezing level, but at high levels, icing may be rime or mixed rime and clear. The abundance of supercooled water makes clear icing very rapid between 0 °C and -15 °C, and encounters can be frequent in a cluster of cells. Thunderstorm icing can be extremely hazardous.

19.6.6 Hail. Hail is precipitation in the form of balls or other irregular lumps of ice produced by thunderstorms. Thunderstorms that are characterized by strong updrafts, large supercooled liquid water contents, large cloud-drop sizes, and great vertical height are favorable to hail formation.

An individual unit of hail is called a hailstone. Hailstones can range in size from a pea (0.25 inch diameter) to larger than a softball (4.5 inch diameter). Hailstones that are 3/4 inch in diameter and larger can cause significant damage to aircraft and make it difficult to control. A hailstone was collected at Vivian, South Dakota, on July 23, 2010, that measured 8 inches in diameter, 18.62 inches in circumference, and weighed 1.93 pounds (see Figure 19-10).

Figure 19-10. Vivian, South Dakota Record Hailstone

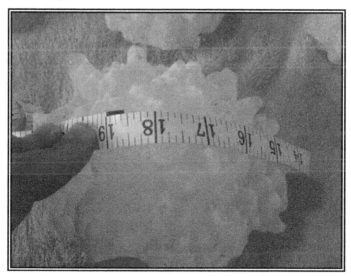

Hail is most frequently found in the interior of continents within the mid-latitudes and generally confined to higher elevations within the tropics. In the United States, hail is most common across the Great Plains region east of the Rocky Mountains. Hail is more common aloft and at higher elevations because the stones begin to melt when they fall below the freezing level, and the smaller stones may melt into raindrops before they reach the surface.

When viewed from the air, it is evident that hail falls in paths known as hail swaths. They can range in size from a few acres to an area 10 miles wide and 100 miles long. Piles of hail in hail swaths have been deep enough to require a snow plow to remove them, and occasionally hail drifts have been reported.

19.6.7 Rapid Altimeter Changes. Pressure usually falls rapidly with the approach of a thunderstorm, then rises sharply with gust frontal passage and arrival of heavy rain showers in the cold downdraft, falling back to normal as the storm moves away. This cycle of pressure change may occur in as little as 15 minutes.

19.6.8 Static Electricity. Static electricity, a steady, high level of noise in radio receivers, is caused by intense corona discharges from sharp metallic points and edges of flying aircraft. It is encountered often in the vicinity of thunderstorms. When an aircraft flies through clouds, precipitation, or a concentration of solid particles (e.g., ice, sand, or dust), it accumulates a charge of static electricity. The electricity discharges onto a nearby surface or into the air, causing a noisy disturbance at lower frequencies.

The corona discharge is weakly luminous and may be seen at night. Although it has a rather eerie appearance, it is harmless. It was named "St. Elmo's Fire" by Mediterranean sailors, who saw the brushy discharge at the top of ship masts.

19.6.9 Tornado. A tornado is a violently rotating column of air in contact with the ground, either pendant from a cumuliform cloud or underneath a cumuliform cloud, and often (but not always) visible as a funnel cloud. When tornadoes do occur without any visible funnel cloud, debris at the surface is usually the indication of the existence of an intense circulation in contact with the ground. A waterspout is any tornado occurring over a body of water.

Tornadoes can occur almost anywhere in the world, but are most common in the central and eastern United States during spring afternoons and evenings. They typically last only a few minutes and travel a few miles, but can persist for more than 90 minutes and track more than 100 miles in extreme cases.

On a local scale, the tornado is the most intense of all atmospheric circulations. Its vortex is typically a few hundred yards in diameter, but can range in width from less than 10 yards to over 2 miles. Wind speeds are typically estimated on the basis of wind damage using the Enhanced Fujita Scale (Enhanced F Scale) (see Table 19-1).

Table 19-1. Enhanced Fujita Scale (Enhanced F Scale) for Tornado Damage

EF-Rating	Class	3 Second Wind Gust		Description	Relative Frequency
		mph	km/h		
EF-0	Weak	65-85	105-137	Gale	53.5%
EF-1	Weak	86-110	138-177	Weak	31.6%
EF-2	Strong	111-135	178-217	Strong	10.7%
EF-3	Strong	136-165	218-266	Severe	3.4%
EF-4	Violent	166-200	267-322	Devastating	0.7%
EF-5	Violent	>200	>322	Incredible	<0.1%

Note: The Enhanced F Scale is a set of wind estimates (not measurements) based on damage. The 3 second gust is not the same wind as in METAR/SPECI surface observations.

Note: Confirmed tornadoes with no reported damage (i.e., those that remain in open fields) are always rated EF-0.

Over 80 percent of all U.S. tornadoes are produced by supercell thunderstorms. Multiple tornado occurrences associated with a particular large-scale weather system is termed a tornado outbreak. On rare occasions, one supercell can produce multiple tornadoes over many hours.

An aircraft entering a tornado is almost certain to suffer structural damage. The tornado vortex has been documented to extend to the cloud top in violent tornadoes.

CHAPTER 20. WEATHER RADAR

20.1 Principles of Weather Radar. The most effective tool to detect precipitation is radar. Radar, which stands for Radio Detection and Ranging, has been utilized to detect precipitation since the 1940s. Radar enhancements have enabled more precision in detecting and displaying precipitation.

The radar used by the National Weather Service (NWS) is called the Weather Surveillance Radar-1988 Doppler (WSR-88D). The prototype radar was built in 1988.

It is essential to understand some principles of weather radar. This will allow you to correctly interpret WSR-88D images. This section will also include a comparison between some WSR-88D principles and aircraft radar principles. These comparisons will help explain the strengths and limitations of the WSR-88D and aircraft radar.

20.1.1 <u>Antenna</u>. The antenna (see Figure 20-1) alternately emits and receives radio waves into the atmosphere. Pulses of energy from the radio waves may strike a target. If it does, part of that energy will return to the antenna.

Figure 20-1. Radar Antenna

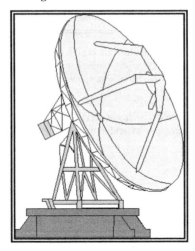

The shape of an antenna determines the shape of a beam. The WSR-88D has a parabolic-shaped antenna. This focuses the radio waves into a narrow, coned-shaped beam. The antenna can be tilted to scan many altitudes of the atmosphere.

20.1.2 <u>Backscattered Energy</u>. The amount of energy returned directly back to the radar after striking a target is called backscattered energy (see Figure 20-2).

Figure 20-2. Backscattered Energy

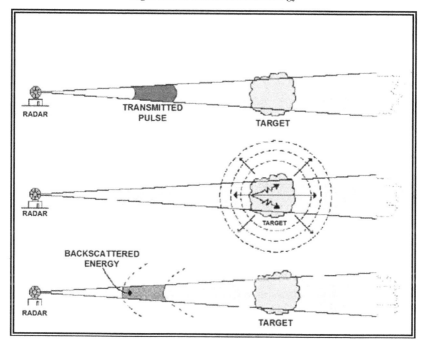

Targets may include precipitation, clouds, dust, birds, insects, buildings, air mass boundaries, terrain features, etc. Reflectivity is a measurement of the amount of backscattered energy. An echo is the appearance, on a radar display, of the backscattered energy (i.e., reflectivity).

20.1.3 Power Output. The WSR-88D has a peak power output of 750 kilowatts. This allows for better detection of low reflectivity (small) targets in the atmosphere, such as clouds, dust, insects, etc.

Most aircraft radar have a peak power output of less than 50 kilowatts. Therefore, smaller targets are difficult to detect with aircraft radar.

20.1.4 Wavelengths. The wavelength is the distance between two crests or two troughs within the radio wave emitted from the radar (see Figure 20-3). The WSR-88D has a wavelength of 10 centimeters. Most aircraft radars have a wavelength of 3 centimeters. Although shorter wavelengths are better at detecting smaller targets, they are significantly more attenuated than longer wavelengths.

Figure 20-3. Wavelengths

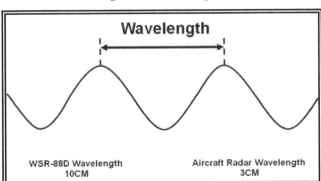

20.1.5 Attenuation. Attenuation is any process which reduces energy within the radar beam. This reduces the amount of backscattered energy.

    20.1.5.1 Precipitation Attenuation. Precipitation attenuation (see Figure 20-4) is the decrease of the intensity of energy within the radar beam due to absorption or scattering of the energy from precipitation particles.

Figure 20-4. Precipitation Attenuation

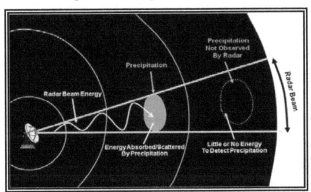

Precipitation close to the radar absorbs and scatters energy within the radar beam. Therefore, very little, if any, energy will reach targets beyond the initial area of precipitation. Because of precipitation attenuation, distant targets (i.e., precipitation) may not be displayed on a radar image.

The amount of precipitation attenuation is related to the wavelength of the radar (see Figure 20-5).

Figure 20-5. Precipitation Attenuation Versus Wavelength

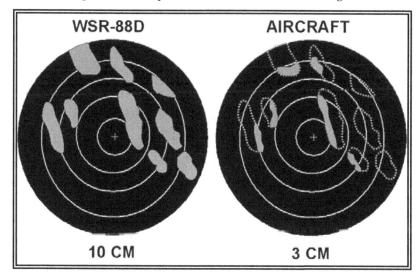

As the wavelength of the radar decreases, the amount of precipitation attenuation increases.

The WSR-88D's 10-centimeter wavelength is not significantly attenuated by precipitation. However, aircraft radars, which typically have 3-centimeter wavelengths, have a significant precipitation attenuation problem. As a result, aircraft weather radar typically only shows the leading edge of extreme intensity echoes.

20.1.5.2 Range Attenuation. Range attenuation is the decrease of the intensity of energy within the radar beam as the beam gets farther away from the antenna. If not compensated for, a target that is farther away from the radar will appear less intense than an identical target closer to the radar.

Range attenuation is automatically compensated for by the WSR-88D. However, most airborne radars only compensate for range attenuation out to a distance of 50 to 75 nautical miles (NM). Targets beyond these ranges will appear less intense than they actually are.

20.1.6 <u>Resolution</u>. Resolution is the ability of the radar to show targets separately.

20.1.6.1 Beam Resolution. Beam resolution is the ability of the radar to identify targets separately at the same range, but different azimuths (see Figure 20-6).

Figure 20-6. Beam Resolution

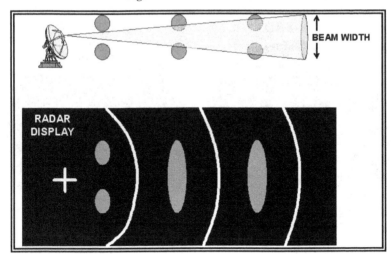

Two targets must be separated by at least one beam width (diameter) in order to be displayed as two separate echoes on a radar image.

The WSR-88D has a beam width of 0.95°. Therefore, at a range of 60 NM, targets separated by at least 1 NM will be displayed separately. At a range of 120 NM, targets separated by at least 2 NM will be displayed separately.

Aircraft radar have beam widths that vary between 3 and 10°. Assuming an average beam width of 5° at a range of 60 NM, targets separated by at least 5.5 NM will be displayed separately. At a range of 120 NM, targets separated by at least 10 NM will be displayed separately.

The beam resolution is better for the WSR-88D than aircraft radar (see Figure 20-7).

Figure 20-7. Beam Resolution Comparison Between WSR-88D and Aircraft Weather Radar

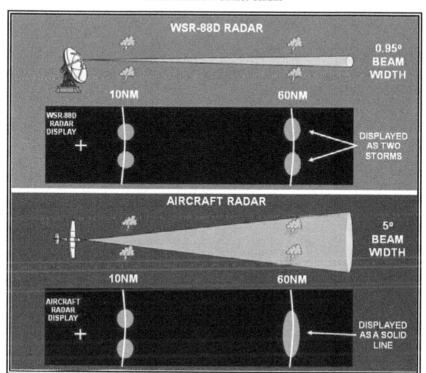

In the example above, the targets (thunderstorms) are at the same range in azimuths for both the aircraft and WSR-88D radar. At 10 NM, the beam width is small enough for both the WSR-88D and aircraft radar to display the thunderstorms separately. At 60 NM, the WSR-88D beam width is still small enough to display both thunderstorms separately. However, the aircraft radar beam width is larger, which results in the two thunderstorms being displayed as one echo.

Note that the beam becomes wider at greater distances from the radar. Therefore, the beam resolution decreases with increasing range from the radar. As a result, lines of precipitation may appear to break up as they move closer to the radar. In reality, the breaks in the precipitation were most likely always there.

20.1.7 Wave Propagation. Radar beams do not travel in a straight line. The beam is bent due to differences in atmospheric density. These density differences, caused by variations in temperature, moisture, and pressure, occur in both the vertical and horizontal directions, and affect the speed and direction of the radar beam.

In a denser atmosphere, the beam travels slower. Conversely, in the less dense atmosphere, the beam travels faster. Changes in density can occur over very small distances, so it is common for the beam to be in areas of different densities at the same time as it gets larger. The beam will bend in the direction of the slower portion of the wave.

20.1.7.1 Normal (Standard) Refraction. Under normal (i.e., standard) conditions, the atmosphere's density gradually decreases with increasing height. As a result, the upper portion of a radar beam travels faster than the lower portion of the beam. This causes the beam to bend downward (see Figure 20-8).

Figure 20-8. Normal Refraction

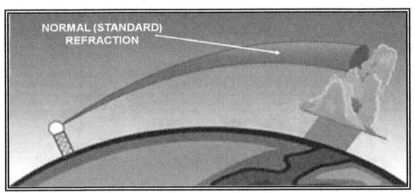

The radar beam curvature is less than the curvature of the Earth. Therefore, the height of the radar beam above the Earth's surface increases with an increasing range.

20.1.7.2 Subrefraction. Atmospheric conditions are never normal or standard. Sometimes, the density of the atmosphere decreases with height at a more than normal rate. When this occurs, the radar beam bends less than normal. This phenomenon is known as subrefraction (see Figure 20-9).

Figure 20-9. Subrefraction

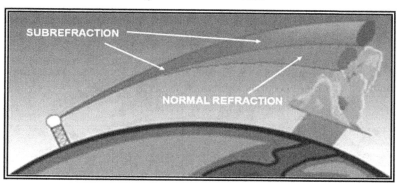

Subrefraction may cause the radar beam to overshoot objects that would normally be detected. For example, distant thunderstorms may not be detected with subrefraction. Subrefraction may also cause radar to underestimate the true strength of a thunderstorm. Thunderstorms may appear weaker on radar because subrefraction causes the radar beam to strike the thunderstorm near the top of the cumulonimbus cloud, where the precipitation particles tend to be smaller.

20.1.7.3 **Superrefraction.** Conversely, sometimes the density of the atmosphere decreases with height at a less than normal rate, or even increases with height. When this occurs, the radar beam will bend more than normal. This phenomenon is called superrefraction (see Figure 20-10).

Figure 20-10. Superrefraction

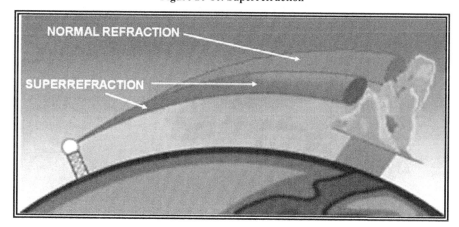

Superrefraction causes the radar beam to travel closer to the Earth's surface than what would occur in a normal atmosphere. This can lead to overestimating the strength of a thunderstorm, as the beam would detect the stronger core of the storm, where precipitation-sized particles are larger.

If the atmospheric condition that causes superrefraction bends the beam equal to, or greater than, the Earth's curvature then a condition called ducting, or trapping, occurs (see Figure 20-11).

Figure 20-11. Ducting

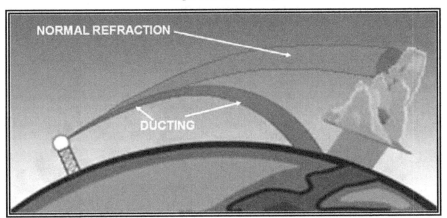

When ducting occurs, the radar beam will hit the surface of the Earth, causing some of the beam's energy to backscatter. This often leads to false echoes, also known as anomalous propagation (AP), to appear in the radar display.

20.1.8 Intensity of Precipitation. The intensity of precipitation is determined from the amount of energy backscattered by precipitation, also known as reflectivity. Reflectivity is determined by:

- The size of precipitation particles;
- The precipitation state (liquid or solid);
- The concentration of precipitation (particles per volume); and
- The shape of the precipitation.

20.1.8.1 **Intensity of Liquid Precipitation.** The most significant factor in determining the reflectivity of liquid particles is the size of the precipitation particle (see Figure 20-12).

Figure 20-12. Reflectivity Associated with Liquid Targets

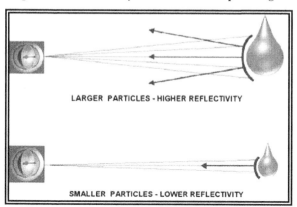

Larger particles have greater reflectivity than smaller particles. For example, a particle with a 1/4-inch diameter backscatters the same amount of energy as 64 particles that each have a 1/8-inch diameter.

Radar images/intensity scales are associated with reflectivities that are measured in decibels of Z (dBZ). The dBZ values increase based on the strength of the return signal from targets in the atmosphere.

Typically, liquid precipitation-sized particle reflectivities are associated with values that are 15 dBZ or greater. Values less than 15 dBZ are typically associated with liquid cloud-sized particles. However, these lower values can also be associated with dust, pollen, insects, or other small particles in the atmosphere.

20.1.8.2 **Intensity of Snow.** A radar image cannot reliably be used to determine the intensity of snowfall. However, in general, snowfall rates generally increase with increasing reflectivity.

20.1.8.3 **Bright Band.** Bright band is a distinct feature observed by radar that denotes the freezing (melting) level. The term originates from a band of enhanced reflectivity that can result when a radar antenna scans through precipitation. The freezing level in a cloud contains ice particles that are coated with liquid water. These particles reflect significantly more energy (appearing to the radar as large raindrops) than the portions of the cloud above and below the freezing layer.

CHAPTER 21. TROPICAL WEATHER

21.1 Circulation. Technically, the Tropics lie between latitudes 23½° N and 23½° S. However, weather typical of this region sometimes extends as much as 45° from the Equator. One may think of the Tropics as uniformly rainy, warm, and humid. The facts are, however, that the Tropics contain both the wettest and driest regions of the world. This chapter describes the basic circulation over the Tropics, terrain influences that determine arid and wet regions, and transitory systems that invade or disturb the basic tropical circulation.

Chapter 4 stated that wind blowing out of the subtropical high pressure belts toward the Equator form the northeast and southeast trade winds of the two hemispheres. These trade winds converge in the vicinity of the Equator where air rises. This convergence zone is the Intertropical Convergence Zone (ITCZ). In some areas of the world, seasonal temperature differences between land and water areas generate rather large circulation patterns that overpower the trade wind circulation; these areas are monsoon regions. Tropical weather discussed here includes the subtropical high pressure belts, the trade wind belts, the ITCZ, and monsoon regions.

21.1.1 Subtropical High Pressure Belts. If the surface under the subtropical high pressure belts were all water of uniform temperature, the high pressure belts would be continuous highs around the globe. The belts would be areas of descending or subsiding air, and would be characterized by strong temperature inversions and very little precipitation. However, land surfaces at the latitudes of the high pressure belts are generally warmer throughout the year than are water surfaces. Thus, the high pressure belts are broken into semi-permanent high pressure areas over oceans with troughs or lows over continents, as shown in Figure 21-1 and Figure 21-2. The subtropical highs shift southward during the Northern Hemisphere winter and northward during summer. The seasonal shift, the height and strength of the inversion, and terrain features determine the weather in the subtropical high pressure belts.

Figure 21-1. Mean Worldwide Surface Pressure Distribution and Prevailing Winds Throughout the World in July

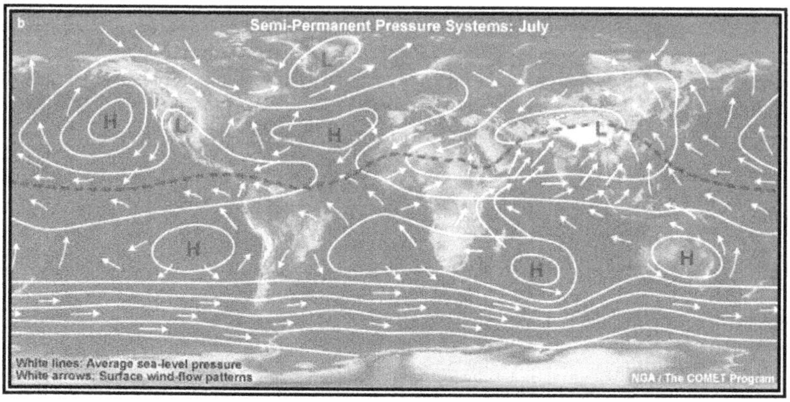

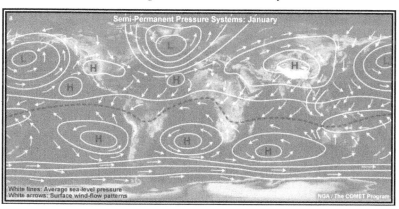

In the warm Northern Hemisphere, warm land areas tend to have low pressure, and cool oceanic areas tend to have high pressure. In the cool Southern Hemisphere, the pattern is reversed: cool land areas tend to have high pressure, and water surfaces have low pressure. However, the relationship is not so evident in the Southern Hemisphere because of relatively small amounts of land. The subtropical high pressure belts are clearly evident at about 30° latitude in both hemispheres. The red dashed line shows the ITCZ.

Figure 21-2. Mean Worldwide Surface Pressure Distribution and Prevailing Winds Throughout the World in January

In this season, the pattern from Figure 21-1 is reversed. In the cool Northern Hemisphere, cold continental areas are predominantly areas of high pressure, while warm oceans tend to be low pressure areas. In the warm Southern Hemisphere, land areas tend to have low pressure, and oceans have high pressure. The subtropical high pressure belts are evident in both hemispheres. Note that the pressure belts shift southward in January and northward in July with the shift in the zone of maximum heating. The red dashed line shows the ITCZ.

21.1.1.1 Continental Weather. Along the west coasts of continents under a subtropical high, the air is stable. The inversion is strongest and lowest where the east side of the subtropical high pressure area overlies the west side of a continent. Moisture is trapped under the inversion; fog and low stratus occur frequently. However, precipitation is rare since the moist layer is shallow and the air is stable. Heavily populated areas also add contaminants to the air which, when trapped under the inversion, add to the visibility problem.

The extreme southwestern United States, for example, is dominated in summer by a subtropical high. We are all familiar with the semiarid summer climate of southern California. Rainfall is infrequent, but fog is common along the coast.

In winter, the subtropical high pressure belts shift southward. Consider southern California as an example. In winter, the area comes under the influence of mid-latitude circulation, which increases frequency of rain. Also, an occasional wintertime outbreak of polar air brings clear skies with excellent visibility.

The situation on eastern continental coasts is just the opposite. The inversion is weakest and highest where the west side of the subtropical high pressure area overlies the eastern coast of a continent. Convection can penetrate the inversion, and showers and thunderstorms often develop. Precipitation is generally sufficient to support considerable vegetation. For example, in the United States, Atlantic coastal areas at the same latitude as southern California are far from arid in summer.

Low ceiling and fog often prevent landing at a west coast destination, but a suitable alternate generally is available a few miles inland. Alternate selection may be more critical for an east coast destination because of widespread instability and associated hazards.

21.1.1.2 Weather over Open Sea. Under a subtropical high over the open sea, cloudiness is scant. The few clouds that do develop have tops from 3,000 to 6,000 feet, depending on height of the inversion. Ceiling and visibility are generally sufficient for visual flight rules (VFR) flight.

21.1.1.3 Island Weather. An island under a subtropical high receives very little rainfall because of the persistent temperature inversion. Surface heating over some larger islands causes light convective showers. Cloud tops are only slightly higher than over open water. Temperatures are mild, showing small seasonal and diurnal changes. A good example is the pleasant, balmy climate of Bermuda.

21.1.2 Trade Wind Belts. Figure 21-1 and Figure 21-2 show prevailing winds throughout the Tropics for July and January. Note that trade winds blowing out of the subtropical highs over ocean areas are predominantly northeasterly in the Northern Hemisphere and southeasterly in the Southern Hemisphere. The inversion from the subtropical highs is carried into the trade winds and is known as the trade wind inversion. As in a subtropical high, the inversion is strongest where the trades blow away from the west coast of a continent and weakest where they blow onto an eastern continental shore. Daily variations from these prevailing directions are small, except during tropical storms. As a result, weather at any specific location in a trade wind belt varies little from day to day.

21.1.2.1 Weather over Open Sea. In the trade wind belt, skies over open water are about one-half covered by clouds on the average. Tops range from 3,000 to 8,000 feet, depending on height of the inversion. Showers, although more common than under a subtropical high, are still light with comparatively little rainfall. Flying weather generally is quite good.

21.1.2.2 Continental Weather. Where trade winds blow offshore along the west coasts of continents, skies are generally clear and the area is quite arid. The Baja Peninsula of Baja California is a well-known example. Where trade winds blow onshore on the east sides of continents, rainfall is generally abundant in showers and occasional thunderstorms. The east coast of Mexico is a good example. Rainfall may be carried a considerable distance inland where the winds are not blocked by a mountain barrier. Inland areas blocked by a mountain barrier are deserts; examples include the Sahara Desert and the arid regions of the southwestern United States. Afternoon convective currents are common over arid regions due to strong surface heating. Cumulus and cumulonimbus clouds can develop, but cloud bases are high, and rainfall is scant because of the low moisture content.

Flying weather along eastern coasts and mountains is subject to the usual hazards of showers and thunderstorms. Flying over arid regions is good most of the time, but can be turbulent in afternoon convective currents; be especially aware of dust devils. Blowing sand or dust sometimes restricts visibility.

21.1.2.3 Island Weather. Mountainous islands have the most dramatic effect on trade wind weather. Since trade winds are consistently from approximately the same direction, they always strike the same side of the island; this side is the windward side. The opposite side is the leeward side. Winds blowing up the windward side produce copious and frequent rainfall, although cloud tops rarely exceed 10,000 feet. Thunderstorms are rare. Downslope winds on the leeward slopes dry the air leaving relatively clear skies and much less rainfall. Many islands in the trade wind belt have lush vegetation and even rain forests on the windward side while the leeward is semiarid. For example, the island of Oahu, Hawaii, is about 24 miles wide in the direction of the trade winds. Annual rainfall averages from about 60 inches on the windward coast to 200 inches at the mountaintops, decreasing to 10 inches on the leeward shore.

The greatest flying hazard near these islands is obscured mountaintops. Ceiling and visibility occasionally restrict VFR flight on the windward side in showers. Instrument flight rules (IFR) weather is virtually nonexistent on leeward slopes.

Islands without mountains have little effect on cloudiness and rainfall. Afternoon surface heating increases convective cloudiness slightly, but shower activity is light. However, any island in either the subtropical high pressure belt or trade wind belt enhances cumulus development even though tops do not reach great heights. Therefore, a cumulus top higher than the average tops of surrounding cumulus usually marks the approximate location of an island. If it becomes necessary for a pilot to ditch in the ocean, he or she should look for, and head toward, a tall cumulus. It probably marks a land surface, increasing chances of survival.

21.1.3 <u>The Intertropical Convergence Zone (ITCZ)</u>. Converging winds in the ITCZ force air upward. The ITCZ appears as a band of clouds consisting of showers, with occasional thunderstorms, that encircles the globe near the Equator. The solid band of clouds may extend for many hundreds of miles and is sometimes broken into smaller line segments. It exists because of the convergence of the trade winds. In the Northern Hemisphere, the trade winds move in a southwesterly direction, while in the Southern Hemisphere they move northwesterly. The tendency for convective storms in the tropics is to be short in their duration, usually on a small scale, but they can produce intense rainfall. It is estimated that 40 percent of all tropical rainfall rates exceed 1 inch per hour. Greatest rainfall typically occurs during midday. On the Equator, this occurs twice a year in March and September, and consequently there are two wet and two dry seasons.

Figure 21-1 and Figure 21-2 show the ITCZ and its seasonal shift. The ITCZ is well-marked over tropical oceans, but is weak and ill-defined over large continental areas.

Convection in the ITCZ carries huge quantities of moisture to great heights. Showers and thunderstorms frequent the ITCZ, and tops to 40,000 feet or higher are common, as shown in Figure 21-1. Precipitation is copious. Since convection dominates the ITCZ, there is little difference in weather over islands and open sea under the ITCZ.

Flying through the ITCZ usually presents no great problem if one follows the usual practice of avoiding cumulonimbus clouds and any thunderstorms.

Since the ITCZ is ill-defined over continents, we will not attempt to describe ITCZ continental weather as such. Continental weather ranges from arid to rain forests and is more closely related to the monsoon than to the ITCZ.

21.1.4 <u>Monsoon</u>. As shown in Figure 21-1 and Figure 21-2, over the large land mass of Asia, the subtropical high pressure breaks down completely. Asia is covered by an intense high during the winter and a well-developed low during the summer. The same occurs over

Australia and central Africa, although the seasons are reversed in the Southern Hemisphere.

The cold, high pressures in winter cause wind to blow from the deep interior outward and offshore. In summer, wind direction reverses, and warm moist air is carried far inland into the low pressure area. This large scale seasonal wind shift is the monsoon. The most notable monsoon is that of southern and southeastern Asia.

21.1.4.1 Summer or Wet Monsoon Weather. During the summer, the low over central Asia draws warm, moist, and unstable maritime air from the southwest over the continent. Strong surface heating, coupled with rising of air flowing up the higher terrain, produces extensive cloudiness, copious rain, and numerous thunderstorms. Rainfall at some stations in India exceeds 400 inches per year with highest amounts between June and October.

The monsoon is so pronounced that it influences circulation many miles out over the ocean. Note in Figure 21-1 that in summer, prevailing winds from the Equator to the south Asian coast are southerly and southeasterly; without the monsoon influence, these areas would be dominated by northeasterly trades. Islands within the monsoon influence receive frequent showers.

21.1.4.2 Winter Monsoon Weather. Note in Figure 21-2 how the winter flow has reversed from that shown in Figure 21-1. Cold, dry air from the high plateau deep in the interior warms adiabatically as it flows down the southern slopes of the Himalayan Mountains. Virtually no rain falls in the interior in the dry winter monsoon. As the dry air moves offshore over warmer water, it rapidly takes in more moisture, becomes warmer in low levels, and, therefore, unstable. Rain is frequent over offshore islands and even along coastal areas after the air has had a significant overwater trajectory.

The Philippine Islands are in an area of special interest. During the summer, they are definitely in southerly monsoon flow and are subjected to abundant rainfall. In the winter, wind over the Philippines is northeasterly—in the transition zone between the northeasterly trades and the monsoon flow. It is academic whether we call the phenomenon the trade winds or monsoon; in either case, it produces abundant rainfall. The Philippines have a year-round humid, tropical climate.

21.1.4.3 Other Monsoon Areas. Australia in July (Southern Hemisphere winter) is an area of high pressure with predominantly offshore winds, as shown in Figure 21-1. Most of the continent is dry during the winter. In January, winds are onshore into the continental low pressure, as shown in Figure 21-2. However, most of Australia is rimmed by mountains, and coastal regions are wet where the onshore winds blow up the mountain slopes. The interior is arid where downslope winds are warmed and dried.

Central Africa is known for its humid climate and jungles. Note in Figure 21-1 and Figure 21-2 that prevailing wind is onshore much of the year over these regions. Some regions are wet year-round; others have the seasonal monsoon shift and have a summer wet season and a winter dry season. Climate of Africa is so varied that only a detailed area-by-area study can explain the climate typical of each area.

In the Amazon Valley of South America during the Southern Hemisphere winter (July), southeast trades, as shown in Figure 21-1, penetrate deep into the valley, bringing abundant rainfall which contributes to the jungle climate. In January, the ITCZ moves south of the valley, as shown in Figure 21-2. The northeast trades are caught up in the monsoon, cross the Equator, and also penetrate the Amazon Valley. The jungles of the Amazon result largely from monsoon winds.

21.1.4.4   Flying Weather in Monsoons. During the winter monsoon, excellent flying weather prevails over dry interior regions. Over water, pilots must pick their way around showers and thunderstorms. In the summer monsoon, VFR flight over land is often restricted by low ceilings and heavy rain. IFR flight must cope with the hazards of thunderstorms. The freezing level in the Tropics is quite high (14,000 feet or higher), so icing is restricted to high levels.

21.2   Transitory Systems. Prevailing circulations are not the only consideration in analyzing weather. Just as important, are migrating tropical weather producers—the shear line, the Tropical Upper Tropospheric Trough (TUTT), tropical waves, areas of converging northeast and southeast trade winds along the ITCZ, and tropical cyclones.

21.2.1   Remnants of Polar Fronts and Shear Lines. Remnants of a polar front can become lines of convection and occasionally generate a tropical cyclone. By the time a cold air mass originating in high latitudes reaches the Tropics, temperature and moisture are virtually the same on both sides of the front. A shear line, or wind shift, is all that remains (see Figure 21-3). These mainly influence storms in the Atlantic Ocean, Gulf of Mexico, or Caribbean Sea early or late in the hurricane season.

Figure 21-3. A Shear Line and an Induced Trough Caused by a Polar High Pushing into the Subtropics

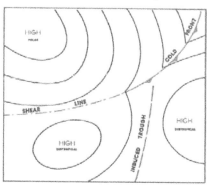

A shear line, also shown in Figure 21-3, results when a semi-permanent high splits into two cells, inducing a trough. These shear lines are zones of convergence creating forced upward motion. Consequently, considerable thunderstorm and rain shower activity occurs along a shear line.

21.2.2 Tropical Upper Tropospheric Trough (TUTT). Troughs above the surface, generally at or above 10,000 feet, move through the Tropics, especially along the poleward fringes. These are known as TUTTs. Figure 21-4 shows such a trough. As a TUTT moves to the southeast or east, it spreads middle and high cloudiness over extensive areas to the east of the trough line. Occasionally, a well-developed trough will extend deep into the Tropics, and a closed low forms at the equatorial end of the trough. The low then may separate from the trough and move westward, producing a large amount of cloudiness and precipitation. If this occurs in the vicinity of a strong subtropical jet stream, extensive, and sometimes dense cirrus and some convective and clear air turbulence, often develop.

Figure 21-4. A TUTT Moves Eastward Across the Hawaiian Islands. Extensive Cloudiness Develops East of the Trough

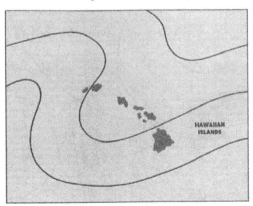

TUTTs and lows aloft produce considerable amounts of rainfall in the Tropics, especially over land areas where mountains and surface heating lift air to saturation. Low pressure systems aloft contribute significantly to the 300+ inches of annual rainfall over the higher terrain of Maui and the big island of Hawaii. Other mountainous areas of the Tropics are also among the wettest spots on Earth.

21.2.3 Tropical Wave. Tropical waves (also called easterly waves) are common tropical weather disturbances, normally occurring in the trade wind belt. In the Northern Hemisphere, they usually develop in the southeastern perimeter of the subtropical high pressure systems. They travel from east to west around the southern fringes of these highs in the prevailing easterly circulation of the Tropics. Surface winds in advance of a wave are somewhat more northerly than the usual trade wind direction. As shown in Figure 21-5, as the wave approaches, pressure falls; as it passes, surface wind shifts to the east-southeast or southeast. The typical wave is preceded by very good weather, but followed by extensive cloudiness (see Figure 21-6), and often by rain and thunderstorms. The weather activity is roughly in a north-south line.

Figure 21-5. A Northern Hemisphere Easterly Wave Progressing from A–B

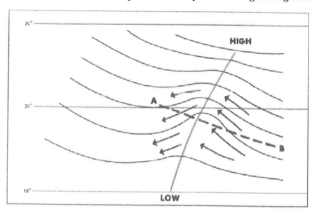

Note that winds shift generally from northeasterly to southeasterly. The wave moves toward the west, and is often preceded by good weather and followed by extensive cloudiness and precipitation.

Figure 21-6. Vertical Cross Section along Line A–B in Figure 21-5

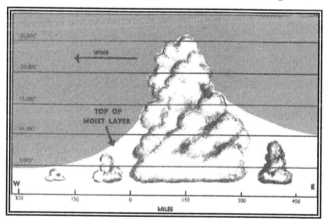

Tropical waves occur in all seasons, but are more frequent and stronger during summer and early fall. Pacific waves frequently affect Hawaii; Atlantic waves occasionally move into the Gulf of Mexico, reaching the U.S. coast.

21.2.4 West African Disturbance Line (WADL). On occasion, a line of convection similar to a squall line moves westward off the continent at tropical latitudes into the oceanic trade winds. In the North Atlantic this is known as the West African Disturbance Line (WADL). A WADL can move faster than easterly waves at 20-40 mph. Some WADLs eventually develop into tropical storms or hurricanes.

21.2.5 Tropical Cyclones. Tropical cyclone is a general term for any low that originates over tropical oceans. Tropical cyclones are classified according to their intensity based on the average 10-minute wind speeds. Wind gusts in these storms may be as much as 50 percent higher than the average 10-minute wind speeds. Over the north Atlantic and northeast Pacific Oceans, tropical cyclone classifications are:

1. Tropical Depression—sustained winds up to 34 knots (64 kilometers per hour).
2. Tropical Storm—sustained winds of 35 to 64 knots (65 to 119 kilometers per hour).
3. Hurricane—sustained winds of at least 65 knots (120 kilometers per hour), or more.

In other regions of the world, different terms are used for tropical cyclones meeting hurricane strength, such as typhoon in the northwest Pacific, severe tropical cyclone in the southwest Pacific and southeast Indian Oceans (e.g., near Australia), severe cyclonic storm in the north Indian Ocean, and just tropical cyclone in the southwest Indian Ocean. The term super typhoon is used if the maximum sustained winds are at least 130 knots (241 kilometers per hour).

21.2.5.1 Development. The prerequisites to tropical cyclone development are optimum sea surface temperature under low-level convergence and cyclonic wind shear. Favored breeding grounds are: shear lines, TUTTs, tropical waves, and lines of convection in low latitudes moving from the continent to the tropical ocean (e.g., WADL).

The low-level convergence associated with these systems by itself will not support development of a tropical cyclone. The system must also have horizontal outflow (divergence) at high tropospheric levels. This combination creates a chimney, in which air is forced upward causing clouds and precipitation. Condensation releases large quantities of latent heat which raises the temperature of the system and accelerates the upward motion. The rise in temperature lowers the surface pressure, which increases low-level convergence. This draws more moisture-laden air into the system. When these chain-reaction events continue, a huge vortex is generated which may culminate in hurricane force winds.

Figure 21-7 shows regions of the world where tropical cyclones frequently develop. Notice that they usually originate between latitudes 5° and 20°. Tropical cyclones are unlikely within 5° of the Equator because the Coriolis force is so small near the Equator that it will not turn the winds enough for them to flow around a low pressure area. Winds flow directly into an equatorial low and rapidly fill it.

Figure 21-7. The Tracks of Nearly 150 Years of Tropical Cyclones and their Strength Weave Across the Globe

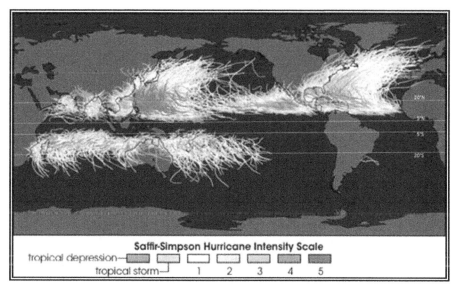

The map is based on all storm tracks available from the National Hurricane Center (NHC) and the Joint Typhoon Warning Center (JTWC) through September 2006. The accumulation of tracks reveals several details of hurricane climatology, such as where the most severe storms form and the large-scale atmospheric patterns that influence the track of hurricanes (from National Aeronautics and Space Administration (NASA)).
Note: See Table 21-1 for wind strength associated with each scale on the Saffir-Simpson Scale).

21.2.5.2 **Movement.** Tropical cyclones in the Northern Hemisphere usually move in a direction between west and northwest while in low latitudes. As these storms move toward the mid-latitudes, they come under the influence of the prevailing westerlies. At this time the storms are under the influence of two wind systems: the trade winds at low levels and prevailing westerlies aloft. Thus, a storm may move very erratically, and may even reverse course or circle. Finally, the prevailing westerlies gain control, and the storm recurves toward the north, then to the northeast, and finally to the east-northeast. By this time, the storm is well into mid-latitudes.

21.2.5.3 **Decay.** As the storm curves toward the north or east (Northern Hemisphere), it usually begins to lose its tropical characteristics and acquires characteristics of lows in middle latitudes. Cooler air flowing into the storm gradually weakens it. If the storm tracks along a coastline or over the open sea, it gives up slowly, carrying its fury to areas far removed from the Tropics. However, if the storm moves well inland, it loses its moisture source and weakens from starvation and increased surface friction, usually after leaving a trail of destruction and flooding.

When a storm takes on middle latitude characteristics, it is said to be extratropical, meaning "outside the Tropics." Tropical cyclones produce weather conditions that differ somewhat from those produced by their higher latitude cousins and invite our investigation.

21.2.5.4 Weather in a Tropical Depression. While in its initial developing stage, the cyclone is characterized by a circular area of broken to overcast clouds in multiple layers. Embedded in these clouds are numerous showers and thunderstorms. Rain shower and thunderstorm coverage varies from scattered to almost solid. Diameter of the cloud pattern varies from less than 100 miles in small systems to well over 200 miles in large ones.

21.2.5.5 Weather in Tropical Storms and Hurricanes. As cyclonic flow increases, the thunderstorms and rain showers form into broken or solid lines, paralleling the wind flow that is spiraling into the center of the storm. These lines are the spiral rain bands frequently seen on radar. These rain bands continually change as they rotate around the storm. Rainfall in the rain bands is very heavy, reducing ceiling and visibility to near zero. Winds are usually very strong and gusty and, consequently, generate violent turbulence. Between the rain bands, ceilings and visibilities are somewhat better, and turbulence generally is less intense.

Most tropical cyclones that form eyes do so within 48 hours of the cyclone reaching tropical storm strength. In the eye, skies are free of turbulent cloudiness, and wind is comparatively light. The average diameter of the eye is between 15 and 20 miles, but sometimes is as small as 7 miles and rarely is more than 30 miles in diameter. Surrounding the eye is a wall of cloud that may extend above 50,000 feet. This wall cloud contains deluging rain and the strongest winds of the storm. Maximum wind speeds of 175 knots have been recorded in some storms. See Figure 21-8 and Figure 21-9 below, which contain a radar display and satellite photograph of a mature hurricane, respectively. Note the spiral rain bands and the circular eye. Notice the similarity between these two figures.

Table 21-1 identifies the wind speed and characteristic house damage for each level on the Saffir-Simpson Hurricane Wind Scale.

Figure 21-8. Radar Image of Hurricane Katrina Observed at New Orleans, Louisiana, on August 29, 2005

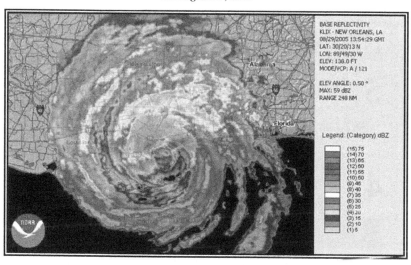

Figure 21-9. Hurricane Andrew Observed by Satellite in 1992

Table 21-1. Wind Speed and Characteristic House Damage for the Saffir-Simpson Hurricane Wind Scale

Saffir-Simpson Hurricane Wind Scale	Wind speed	Characteristic House Damage
5	≥157 mph ≥137 knots ≥252 km/h	Almost complete destruction of all mobile homes will occur, regardless of age or construction A high percentage of frame homes will be destroyed, with total roof failure and wall collapse. Extensive damage to roof covers, windows, and doors will occur. Large amounts of windborne debris will be lofted into the air. Windborne debris damage will occur to nearly all unprotected windows and many protected windows.
4	130-156 mph 113-136 knots 209-251 km/h	Nearly all older (pre-1994) mobile homes will be destroyed. A high percentage of newer mobile homes also will be destroyed. Poorly constructed frame homes can sustain complete collapse of all walls as well as the loss of the roof structure. Well-built homes also can sustain severe damage with loss of most of the roof structure and/or some exterior walls. Extensive damage to roof coverings, windows, and doors will occur. Large amounts of windborne debris will be lofted into the air. Windborne debris damage will break most unprotected windows and penetrate some protected windows.
3	111-129 mph 96-112 knots 178-208 km/h	Nearly all older (pre-1994) mobile homes will be destroyed. Most newer mobile homes will sustain severe damage with potential for complete roof failure and wall collapse. Poorly constructed frame homes can be destroyed by the removal of the roof and exterior walls. Unprotected windows will be broken by flying debris. Well-built frame homes can experience major damage involving the removal of roof decking and gable ends.
2	96-110 mph 83-95 knots 154-177 km/h	Older (mainly pre-1994 construction) mobile homes have a very high chance of being destroyed, and the flying debris generated can shred nearby mobile homes. Newer mobile homes can also be destroyed. Poorly constructed frame homes have a high chance of having their roof structures removed, especially if they are not anchored properly. Unprotected windows will have a high probability of being broken by flying debris. Well-constructed frame homes could sustain major roof and siding damage. Failure of aluminum, screened-in, swimming pool enclosures will be common.
1	74-95 mph 64-82 knots 119-153 km/h	Older (mainly pre-1994 construction) mobile homes could be destroyed, especially if they are not anchored properly as they tend to shift or roll off their foundations. Newer mobile homes that are anchored properly can sustain damage involving the removal of shingle or metal roof coverings, and loss of vinyl siding, as well as damage to carports, sunrooms, or lanais. Some poorly constructed frame homes can experience major damage, involving loss of the roof covering and damage to gable ends, as well as the removal of porch coverings and awnings. Unprotected windows may break if struck by flying debris. Masonry chimneys can be toppled. Well--constructed frame homes could have damage to roof shingles, vinyl siding, soffit panels, and gutters. Failure of aluminum, screened-in, swimming pool enclosures can occur.

CHAPTER 22. ARCTIC WEATHER

22.1 **Introduction.** Strictly speaking, the Arctic is the region shown below in Figure 22-1, which lies within the Arctic Circle (66.5° N latitude). However, it is loosely defined as the northern regions, in general. This chapter includes Alaskan weather, even though much of Alaska lies south of the Arctic Circle.

As an introduction to Arctic weather, this chapter surveys climate, air masses, and fronts of the Arctic, introduces you to some Arctic weather peculiarities, and discusses weather hazards in the Arctic.

Figure 22-1. The Arctic Circle

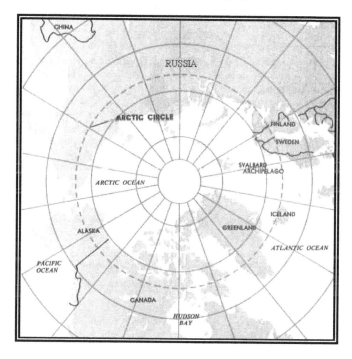

22.2 **Climate, Air Masses, and Fronts.** There are a number of factors that influence Arctic climate. Climate of any region, especially in the Arctic, is largely determined by the amount of energy received from the sun; however, local characteristics of the area, such as mountains and ice cover, also influence climate.

22.2.1 Long Days and Nights. A profound seasonal change in length of day and night occurs in the Arctic because of the Earth's tilt and its revolution around the sun. Any point north of the Arctic Circle has fall and winter days when the sun stays below the horizon all day and has spring and summer days with 24 hours of sunshine when the sun stays above the horizon. The number of these days increases toward the North Pole; there the sun stays below the horizon for 6 months and shines continuously during the other 6 months.

Twilight in the Arctic is prolonged because of the shallow angle of the sun below the horizon. In more northern latitudes, it persists for days when the sun remains just below the horizon. This abundance of twilight often makes visual reference possible at night.

22.2.2 Land and Water. Figure 22-1 shows the water and the land distribution in the Arctic. Arctic mountain ranges are effective barriers to air movement. Large masses of air stagnate over inland continental areas; thus, Arctic continental areas are air mass source regions.

A large portion of the Arctic Ocean is covered throughout the year by a deep layer of ice, known as the permanent ice pack. This ice pack goes through a seasonal cycle where ice melts in the spring and summer and increases in the fall and winter. Even though a large portion of the Arctic Ocean is ice-covered through much of the year, the ice and the water below contain more heat than the surrounding cold land, thus moderating the climate. Oceanic and coastal areas have a milder climate during winter and a cool climate in summer. As opposed to large water bodies, large land areas show a more significant seasonal temperature variation.

22.2.3 Temperature. As one would expect, the Arctic is very cold in winter, but due to local terrain and the movement of pressure systems, occasionally some areas are surprisingly warm. During winter, coastal areas are warmer than the interior. During summer, interior areas are pleasantly warm due to many hours of sunshine, while coastal areas have relatively short, cool summers due to their proximity to water.

22.2.4 Clouds and Precipitation. Cloudiness over the Arctic is at a minimum during winter due to the ice pack being more widespread. Spring brings many cloudy days, with cloudiness reaching a maximum in summer and fall when a portion of the sea ice melts and exposes additional water in the Arctic Ocean.

During summer afternoons, scattered cumulus clouds forming over the interior occasionally grow into thundershowers. These thundershowers move generally from northeast to southwest in the polar easterlies, which is opposite the general movement in the mid-latitudes.

During the winter, polar lows can form over the open ocean. Polar lows are small, intense low-pressure systems that can develop rapidly when cold air flows over warm water. They produce severe weather, strong surface winds, and heavy precipitation. Polar lows dissipate quickly once they move over land.

Precipitation in the Arctic can vary drastically per region, but is generally light. Some areas are known as polar deserts. In winter, the only precipitation received in the Arctic is snow, while in summer precipitation falls mostly in the form of snow over ice caps and oceanic areas and rain over interior areas. Annual amounts of precipitation over the ice pack and along the coastal areas tend to be less than the interior areas.

22.2.5 Wind. Typically, Arctic winds are light. Strong winds occur more often along the coastal areas in fall and winter. Wind speeds are generally light in the continental interior throughout the entire year, but are normally at their strongest during summer and fall.

22.2.6 Air Masses—Winter. In winter, air masses form over the expanded ice pack and adjoining snow-covered land areas. These air masses are characterized by very cold surface air, very low humidity, and strong low-level temperature inversions. Occasionally, air from unfrozen ocean areas flows northward over the Arctic. These intrusions of moist, cold air account for most of the infrequent wintertime cloudiness and precipitation in the Arctic.

22.2.7 Air Masses—Summer. During the summer, the top layer of the Arctic permafrost layer melts, leaving very moist ground, and the open water areas of the Polar Basin increase markedly. Thus, the entire area becomes more humid, relatively mild, and semi-maritime in character. The largest amounts of cloudiness and precipitation occur inland during the summer months.

22.2.8 Fronts. Occluded fronts are the rule. Weather conditions with occluded fronts are much the same in the Arctic as elsewhere: low clouds, precipitation, poor visibility, and sudden fog formation. Fronts are much more frequent over coastal areas than over the interior.

22.3 **Arctic Peculiarities.** Several Arctic phenomena are peculiar to the region.

22.3.1 Effects of Temperature Inversion. The Arctic experiences frequent low-level temperature inversions, which occur when temperature increases with height (i.e., cold air settled near the ground with warm air directly above). Inversions can slow down surface winds and trap pollutants, creating smoggy and hazy conditions that persist until the inversion ends. In addition, light rays are bent as they pass at low angles through the inversion, creating an effect known as looming, which is a form of mirage that causes objects beyond the horizon to appear above the horizon. These low-level inversion mirages distort the shape of the sun, moon, and other objects.

22.3.2 Light Reflection by Snow-Covered Surfaces. Much more light is reflected by snow-covered surfaces than by darker surfaces. Snow often reflects Arctic sunlight sufficiently to blot out shadows, thus decreasing the contrast between objects. Dark, distant mountains may be easily recognized, but a crevasse normally directly in view may be undetected due to lack of contrasts.

22.3.3 Light from Celestial Bodies. Illumination from the moon and stars is much more intense in the Arctic than in lower latitudes. Even illumination from the stars creates visibility far beyond that found elsewhere. Only under heavy overcast skies does the night darkness in the Arctic begin to approach the degree of darkness in lower latitudes.

22.4 Weather Hazards.
Weather hazards include visibility restricting phenomena, blowing snow, icing, frost, and lack of contrast (whiteout).

22.4.1 Fog and Ice Fog.
Fog occurs when water droplets or ice particles are suspended in the air at the Earth's surface. Water-droplet fog occurs in coastal areas during the summer. Ice fog (also called ice-crystal fog, frozen fog, frost fog, frost flakes, air hoar, rime fog, and pogonip) is a type of fog formed by direct freezing of supercooled water droplets. Ice fog is composed of suspended particles of ice, partly ice crystals 20-100 micron in diameter, but chiefly (especially when dense) ice particles about 12-20 micron in diameter. It occurs at very low temperatures, and usually in clear, calm weather in high latitudes. The sun may cause the appearance of a halo. Effective visibility is reduced considerably more when looking toward the sun. Ice fog is rare at temperatures warmer than -30 °C, and increases in frequency with decreasing temperature until it is almost always present at air temperatures of -45 °C in the vicinity of a source of water vapor. Such sources of water vapor are the open water of fast-flowing streams or of the sea, herds of animals, volcanoes, and especially products of combustion for heating, automobiles, and aircraft. At temperatures warmer than -30 °C, these sources can cause steam fog of liquid water droplets, which may turn into ice fog when cooled.

22.4.2 Blowing and Drifting Snow.
Over the frozen Arctic Ocean and along the coastal areas, blowing snow, drifting snow, and strong winds are common hazards during fall and winter. Blowing snow is wind-driven falling or accumulated snow that reduces surface visibility. Drifting snow is an uneven distribution of snowfall or snow depth caused by strong surface winds, which may occur during or after a snowfall. Drifting snow is usually associated with blowing snow. In the Arctic, because the snow is dry and fine, it can be picked up easily by light winds that raise the snow several feet off the ground, obliterating objects. A sudden increase in surface wind may cause an unlimited visibility to drop to near zero in a few minutes. This sudden loss of visibility occurs frequently without warning in the Arctic.

22.4.3 Frost.
Frost is the formation of thin ice crystals on the ground or other surfaces on solid objects below the freezing point of water. It develops in Arctic coastal areas during spring, fall, and winter.

22.4.4 Whiteout.
Whiteout is a visibility-restricting phenomenon that occurs most often in the spring and fall in the Arctic when the sun is near the horizon. It occurs when a layer of overcast clouds overlies a snow- or ice-covered surface. Parallel rays of the sun are broken up and diffused when passing through the cloud layer so that they strike the snow surface from many angles. The diffused light then reflects back and forth countless times between the snow and the cloud, eliminating all shadows. The result is a loss of depth perception. Buildings, people, and dark-colored objects appear to float in the air, and the horizon disappears.

CHAPTER 23. SPACE WEATHER

23.1 The Sun—Prime Source of Space Weather. The sun is the dominant source of the conditions commonly described as space weather. The term space weather is used to designate processes occurring on the sun and in Earth's magnetosphere, ionosphere, and thermosphere, which have the potential to affect the near-Earth environment. Emissions from the sun are both continuous (e.g., solar luminescence and solar wind) and eruptive (e.g., coronal mass ejections (CME) and flares). These solar eruptions may cause radio blackouts, magnetic storms, ionospheric storms, and radiation storms at Earth.

Similar to the charged particles that come from the sun, Galactic Cosmic Rays (GCR) are charged particles that originate in more distant supernovae and contribute to the space weather conditions near Earth. Essentially, these charged particles comprise a steady drizzle of radiation at Earth.

The sum of the solar and nonsolar components equal the full extent of the potential radiation dose received. The size of the GCR flux varies inversely with the sunspot cycle (sunspots are described in later paragraphs); that is, during sunspot minimums when the interplanetary environment near Earth is laminar and steady, the GCR component is large due to its easier access to the near-Earth environment. At sunspot maximum, the turbulence and energetics associated with solar eruptions reduce GCR access to the vicinity of the Earth.

23.2 The Sun's Energy Output and Variability. The sun is a variable star. That means the balance between the continuous emissions and the eruptive emissions changes with time. One metric that is commonly used to track this variability is the occurrence of sunspots. Astronomers have made sunspot observations continuously for hundreds, maybe even thousands, of years. Though the underlying physics is still not well understood, on average sunspots come and go in an 11-year period. The magnitude and duration of individual cycles varies, but typically more eruptive events occur near the solar maximum, while few are observed near solar minimum. All solar electromagnetic emissions, from radio to x rays, are also stronger during solar maximum and less intense near solar minimum.

23.3 Sunspots and the Solar Cycle. Because space weather activity varies with sunspot activity, they are often used as a proxy index for changing space weather conditions. This is because sunspots, by their very nature, exist due to strong local magnetic fields. When these fields erupt, severe space weather can occur. While sunspots are easily seen, other events such as GCR, CMEs, and increased solar wind are more difficult to observe from the ground and may not be related to long historical records of sunspots.

23.4 Solar Wind. The solar wind is the continuous flow away from the sun of charged particles and magnetic field, called plasma. Solar wind is a consequence of the very high temperature of the solar corona and the resultant expansion of the plasma into space.

The solar wind carries the energy from most solar eruptions that affect the near-Earth environment. The sole exception, solar flare photons consisting of light and x rays, carry the energy released in solar flares. Even in the absence of an eruption, the constant flow of plasma fuels Earth's geomagnetic field. The solar wind may be fast and energetic if an eruption occurs, or can gradually increase due to a coronal-hole structure which allows unimpeded high-speed solar wind to escape from the corona. As seen from the Earth, the sun rotates on approximately a 27-day period, so well-established coronal-hole structures that persist for several months will swing by Earth on schedule, roughly every 27 days.

23.5 Solar Eruptive Activity. Most solar eruptions originate in areas that have strong magnetic fields. Usually marked with sunspots, these areas are commonly called active regions. Active regions are numerous and common during solar maximum and scarce during solar minimum.

Flares and CMEs are the two major types of solar eruptions. They may occur independently or at the same time. Solar flares have been recognized for more than 100 years, as they can be seen from the ground. In the past 50 years, Hydrogen-Alpha (656.3 nanometer wavelength) filter-equipped ground-based telescopes have been used to observe flares.

Flares are characterized by a very bright flash phase which may last for a few minutes to a few hours during the largest flares. Flares can emit at all frequencies across the electromagnetic emission spectrum, from gamma rays to radio.

CMEs, in contrast to solar flares, are difficult to detect, not particularly bright, and may take hours to fully erupt from the sun. CMEs literally are an eruption of a large volume of the solar outer atmosphere, the corona. Prior to the satellite era, they were very difficult to observe. The energy released in a large solar flare is on par with that released in a CME, however CMEs are far more effective in perturbing Earth's magnetic field and are known to cause the strongest magnetic storms. A typical travel time for a CME from the sun to Earth may range from less than 1 day to more than 4 days. The travel time of the electromagnetic emission produced during flares, by comparison, is at the speed of light. They instantaneously affect the dayside of Earth upon observation.

The frequency of solar flares and CMEs tracks with the solar cycle. As many as 25 solar flares may occur per day during the maximum phase of the solar cycle. At solar minimum, it may take 6 months or more for 25 flares to occur. CME frequency varies from about 5 per day near solar maximum to one per week or longer at solar minimum.

Many CMEs observed lifting off the sun are not Earth-directed.

23.6 Geospace. Geospace is the volume of space that surrounds Earth, influenced by the Earth's magnetic field in the solar wind. If Earth did not have a magnetic field, the solar wind would blow past unimpeded, affected only by the mass of Earth and its atmosphere. Earth's magnetic field extends outward in all directions. This forms a cocoon for the planet, protecting it from the flow of the solar wind. The cocoon is called the magnetosphere. The magnetosphere typically extends towards the sun about 10 Earth radii on the dayside and stretches away from the sun many times more on the night side. The shape is similar to a comet tail with it being extended during strong solar wind conditions and less so during more quiet times. On its flanks, the magnetosphere extends outward roughly 20 Earth radii in the dawn and dusk sectors.

The magnetosphere deflects most of the energy carried by the solar wind, while making a fraction of it available to be absorbed by the near-Earth system. When the sun is active and CMEs interact with Earth, the additional energy disrupts the magnetosphere, resulting in a magnetic storm. Then, over time, the magnetosphere adjusts through various processes and once more returns to normal.

The most visible manifestation of the energy being absorbed from the solar wind into the magnetosphere is the aurora, both in the Northern and Southern Hemispheres. The aurora occurs when accelerated electrons from the sun follow the magnetic field of Earth down to the polar regions, where they collide with oxygen and nitrogen atoms and molecules in Earth's upper atmosphere. In these collisions, the electrons transfer their energy to the atmosphere, thus exciting the atoms and molecules to higher energy states. When they relax to lower energy states, they release their energy in the form of light. Simply put, the more energy in the solar wind, the brighter and more widespread the aurora glow becomes.

Nearer to Earth is another region called the ionosphere. It is a shell of weak plasma, where electrons and ions exist embedded in the neutral atmosphere. The ionosphere begins at roughly 80 kilometers in altitude and extends out many Earth radii, at the topside.

Extreme Ultraviolet (EUV) solar emissions create the ionosphere by ionizing the neutral atmosphere. The electrons and ions created by this process then engage in chemical reactions that progress faster in the lower ionosphere. The ionosphere changes significantly from day to night. When the sun sets, chemical processes, together with other dynamic processes, allow some of the ionization to remain until the new day brings the solar EUV once again. An important point is that the energy that comes from the sun in the solar wind makes its way to the ionosphere, where it alters the ambient conditions during space weather storms.

23.7 Galactic Cosmic Radiation. Galactic Cosmic Radiation, more commonly known as Galactic Cosmic Rays (GCR), are a consequence of distant supernovae raining charged particles, heavy ions, protons, and electrons onto the inner heliosphere. The abundance of GCR is inversely rated to the solar cycle. At solar maximum, when the solar wind flow is turbulent and strong, the GCR flux is inhibited and therefore low. At solar minimum, the GCR flux increases by about 30 percent in the near-Earth environment. When high-energy GCR enter Earth's atmosphere, it creates a cascade of interactions resulting in a range of secondary particles, including neutrons that make their way to Earth's surface.

23.8 Geomagnetic Storms. Geomagnetic storms are strong disturbances to Earth's magnetic field in the solar wind. These storms pose problems for many activities, technological systems, and critical infrastructure. The topology of Earth's magnetic field changes in the course of a storm, as the near-Earth system attempts to adjust to the jolt of energy from the sun. CMEs and the shocks they drive are often the causative agent, and can send the geomagnetic field into a disturbed state.

The most obvious, and probably the only pleasing, attribute of an energized geomagnetic field are the auroras. Geomagnetic storms tend to brighten auroras and allow them to move equatorward.

The duration of geomagnetic storms is usually on the order of days. The strongest storms may persist for almost 1 week. A string of CMEs may cause prolonged disturbed periods related to the additional energy being pumped toward the Earth.

Although the frequency of geomagnetic storms reflects the solar cycle, a closer look shows a bimodal distribution. Large numbers of storms cluster at solar maximum resulting from frequent CMEs, and again in the declining phase due to high-speed solar wind streams. Typically, the most intense storms occur near solar maximum, with weaker storms occurring during the declining phase.

23.9 Solar Radiation Storms. Solar radiation storms occur when large quantities of charged particles, primarily protons, are accelerated by processes at or near the sun, then bathe the near-Earth environment with these charged particles. These particles cause an increase in the radiation dose to humans, and increase the possibility of single-event upsets in electronics. Earth's magnetic field and atmosphere offer some protection from this radiation, but protection decreases with altitude, latitude, magnetic field strength, and direction. The polar regions on Earth are most open to these charged particles. The magnetic field lines at the poles extend vertically downwards, intersecting Earth's surface. This allow the particles to spiral down the field lines and penetrate into the atmosphere and increase the ionization.

A significant factor related to the criticality of the radiation increase at Earth is the energy distribution of the solar protons. Protons of varying energies will bathe Earth as a function of the site of the eruption at the sun and the magnetic connection between the sun and Earth. High-energy protons cause radiation dose increases that are of concern to human beings. Lower energy protons have little effect on humans, but have a severe impact on the polar ionosphere.

The duration of solar radiation storms is a function of the magnitude of the solar eruption as well as the energy level of protons. For events that are of a large magnitude but low energy, the duration may last for 1 week. Events that are of high energy may last for only a few hours. There is a great diversity in the duration of solar radiation storms, as there are many factors that contribute to the acceleration and propagation of the charged particles near Earth.

Solar radiation storms can occur at any point in the solar cycle, but tend to be most common during the years around solar maximum.

23.10 Ionospheric Storms. Ionospheric storms arise from large influxes of solar particle and electromagnetic radiation. There is a strong coupling between the ionosphere and the magnetosphere, which means both regimes can be disturbed concurrently.

The symptoms of an ionospheric storm include enhanced currents, turbulence and wave activity, and a nonhomogeneous distribution of free electrons. This clustering of electrons, which leads to scintillation of signals passing through the cluster, is particularly problematic for the Global Navigation Satellite System (GNSS).

The duration of the ionospheric storm impact may range from a few minutes to days-long prolonged events. As a general rule, these ionospheric storms mimic the duration of geomagnetic storms.

The intensity of ionospheric storms varies significantly as a function of local time, season, and time within the solar cycle.

The frequency of occurrence of ionospheric storms is also similar to geomagnetic storms with one important caveat. The near-equatorial ionosphere, a band extending approximately $\perp 10°$ in latitude on either side of the magnetic equator, can be very disturbed in the post-sunset to near-midnight hours, even in the absence of a geomagnetic storm. This behavior is related to the internal electrodynamics of the ionosphere rather than external stimulation from the sun. The disturbance is very difficult to predict and is best described by the climatological statistics for that region.

23.11 Solar Flare Radio Blackouts. Radio blackouts primarily affect high frequency (HF) (3-30 megahertz (MHz)), although detrimental effects may spill over to very high frequency (VHF) (30-300 MHz) and beyond, resulting in fading and diminished ability for reception. The blackouts are a consequence of enhanced electron densities caused by the emissions from solar flares that ionize the sunlit side of Earth.

The process consists of x ray and EUV bursts from a solar flare, increasing the number of free electrons in the atmosphere below 90 kilometers, which in turn increases their interaction with the neutral atmosphere that increases the amount of radio energy lost as radio waves pass through this region. During a large flare event, the amount of radio energy lost is sufficient to make the return signal from the ionosphere too small to be useful with normal radio receivers. The net effect of this process is a blackout for HF transmissions.

The duration of dayside solar flare radio blackouts closely follows the duration of the solar flares that cause them beginning with the arrival of the x ray and EUV photons, and abate with their diminution. Usually, the radio blackouts last for several minutes, but they can last for hours.

23.12 Effects of Space Weather on Aircraft Operations.

23.12.1 <u>Communications</u>. HF communications at low- to mid-latitudes are used by aircraft during transoceanic flights and routes where line-of-sight VHF communication is not an option. HF enables a skip mode to send a signal around the curvature of Earth. HF communications on the dayside can be adversely affected when a solar flare occurs and its photons rapidly alter the electron density of the lower altitudes of the ionosphere, causing fading, noise, or a total blackout. Usually these disruptions are short-lived (tens of minutes to a few hours), so the outage ends fairly quickly.

HF communications at high latitudes and polar regions are adversely affected for longer periods, sometimes days, due to some space weather events. The high latitude and polar ionosphere is a sink for charged particles, which alter the local ionization and provide steep local ionization gradients to deflect HF radio waves, as well as increase local absorption.

Satellite communication signals pass through the bulk of the ionosphere and are a popular means of communicating over a wide area. The frequencies normally used for satellite communications are high enough for the ionosphere to appear transparent. However, when the ionosphere is turbulent and nonhomogeneous, an effect called scintillation, a twinkling in both amplitude and phase, is imposed upon the transmitted signal. Scintillations can result in loss-of-lock and inability for the receiver to track a Doppler-shifted radio wave.

23.12.2 <u>Navigation and Global Positioning System (GPS)</u>. Space weather adversely affects GPS in three ways: it increases the error of the computed position, it causes a loss-of-lock for receivers, and it overwhelms the transmitted signal with solar radio noise.

23.12.3 <u>Radiation Exposure to Flightcrews and Passengers</u>. Solar radiation storms occurring under particular circumstances cause an increase in radiation dose to flightcrews and passengers. As high polar latitudes and high altitudes have the least shielding from the particles, the threat is the greatest for higher altitude polar flights. The increased dose is much less of an issue for low- and mid-latitude flights.

23.12.4 <u>Radiation Effects on Avionics</u>. The electronic components of aircraft avionic systems are susceptible to damage from the highly ionizing interactions of cosmic rays, solar particles, and the secondary particles generated in the atmosphere. As these components become increasingly smaller, and therefore more susceptible, the risk of damage also increases.

Advisory Circular Feedback Form

If you find an error in this AC, have recommendations for improving it, or have suggestions for new items/subjects to be added, you may let us know by contacting the Flight Technologies and Procedures Division (AFS-400) at 9-AWA-AFS400-COORD@faa.gov or the Flight Standards Directives Management Officer at 9 AWA-AFS-140-Directives@faa.gov.

Subject: AC 00-6B, Aviation Weather

Date: _____

Please check all appropriate line items:

☐ An error (procedural or typographical) has been noted in paragraph _____ on page _____.

☐ Recommend paragraph _____ on page _____ be changed as follows:

_____
_____

☐ In a future change to this AC, please cover the following subject:
(*Briefly describe what you want added.*)

_____
_____

☐ Other comments:

_____
_____

☐ I would like to discuss the above. Please contact me.

Submitted by: _____ Date: _____

Made in the USA
Monee, IL
18 January 2020